"This is truly a heroine's journey. Lynne's writing is so clear and concise, I felt as if I were walking with her every step of the way. Her fears, tears, and final triumph were so compelling, I felt like they belonged to me."

–Scott Allan Miller, Registered Nurse and Health Care Consultant

"Lynne captures so beautifully the roller coaster ride of life. Her openness about her experience helped me understand what my late husband went through during four years with leukemia. Lynne brings humor and love into a situation that is anything but normal."

–Nancy Goodson, Wife of cancer victim

"Lynne Massie is an insightful person who inspires her reader to step out of their comfort zone and venture forth upon new avenues of thought and action."

–Joan A. McLaren Henson, Child of God, Poet and Teacher

"This book held me spellbound. Using wit, humor, and compassion, Lynne takes the mystery out of traveling through cancer, both the ugliness and the blessings. She shares, not only her story, but also the journey and transformation of her entire family. Even though I experienced much of this journey with Lynne, I still could not put this compelling book down."

–Victoria Etchemendy, Minister Unity World Healing Center,
Lake Oswego, OR

"*I'll Be Here Tomorrow* is to inspire your soul, tickle your funny bone and motivate your mind to say 'yes' to life. Lynne's journey of survival has gifted us all with her wisdom and courage. If you know anyone who has suffered from a major illness or life challenge, this book is a must-read."

–Jody Miller Stevenson, Author of the popular books
Soul Purpose and Solutions

I'll Be Here Tomorrow

Transforming Tragedy into Triumph

LYNNE MASSIE

CYMITAR INC.
TUMWATER, WA

Published by Cymitar Inc.
855 Trosper Road – #108-310
Tumwater, WA 98512

Publisher's Cataloguing-in-Publication Data
Massie, Lynne.

      I'll be here tomorrow : transforming tragedy into triumph / Lynne Massie. –
      Tumwater, WA : Cymitar Inc., 2004.

      p. ; cm.
      ISBN: 0-9669075-4-X

      1. Massie, Lynne. 2. Terminally ill–Attitudes. 3. Choice (Psychology) 4. Courage. 5. Self-actualization (Psychology) 6. Conduct of life. I. Title.

BF611 .M37 2004   2004109367
153.8/3–dc22   0409

Book production and coordination by Jenkins Group, Inc. • www.bookpublishing.com
Interior production by Barbara Hodge
Cover design by Kelli Leader

COVER ILLUSTRATION
Cover illustration by Connie Bowen, author/illustrator of the best selling affirmation books, "I Turn To The Light" and "I Believe In Me." Both books are for spiritual growth and healing. Visit her Web site at http://www.europa.com/~cbowen or e-mail her at cbowen@europa.com.

Printed in the United States of America
08 07 06 05 04 • 5 4 3 2 1

ACKNOWLEDGMENTS

A big "thank you" to the people below who gave from their hearts:

My children, Dana and Keaton, who endured this illness like troopers, and, of course, my husband, Hal, who has hung in there with me for thirty years–through sickness and health.

My parents, Jean and John Pierson, and my sisters, Anne Ireland and Nancy Goodson, who made the long journey from Georgia just to sit with me during some of my treatments.

Victoria Etchemendy, my minister, who helped me walk down the spiritual path of cancer.

Our family counselor, Nick Kreofsky, who helped us climb over many of the boulders that were in the path of this journey.

Lee Sherry, who stayed the course of friendship through my emotional ups and downs. He has now left this earth and is spending eternity with Ben.

Carolyn Horner and Jody Stevenson, my dear friends, who encouraged me throughout the process of completing this book.

My friends who cooked, cleaned, did laundry, brought me water, and sat by my bedside. And special thanks to Mary Davidson, who tirelessly made arrangements to have meals brought in, drivers take me to and from treatments, and sitters when I was too sick to care for myself.

Dr. Robert Basham, a local psychologist, who spent many hours counseling me, just before and at the time of my diagnosis.

Kay Allenbaugh and Dr. Al Siebert, who, through their own work and publications, inspired me throughout the process of writing this book.

Burky Achilles, who tirelessly and expertly edited the manuscript and put up with me while I delayed, argued, and sometimes doubted her wonderful wisdom. She did a superb job!

Chapter One

S ome days, adversity is nothing more than a minor interference in our daily lives: a heavy traffic jam on the freeway, a burned dinner, a bad winter cold. On other days, life deals heavy blows, and our very survival is at stake. At times like these, often our normal channels of support, while well meaning, are ill equipped to do little more than offer condolences. I know.

My name is Lynne Massie, and often I wonder whether I am a ghost who is just imagining that I have a physical body. I feel I am residing on this planet only in spirit. You see, I am the survivor of not one but two terminal illnesses.

At sixteen, I played sports, lots of them. Hooked on golf at ten, I added softball in junior high and then tennis and basketball in high school. In late August before my junior year, I even took up water skiing.

Every new sport brings its attendant aches and pains, so I didn't think much of the initial stiffness in my arms and back or the continuous burn in my legs. I was sure it would pass, and I'd be fine. But by the third day, the pain worsened. "Probably just growing pains," my mother said. "Take some aspirin."

I downed aspirin on the fourth, fifth, and sixth days. I took it before breakfast even though it made my stomach queasy, and I took it again a couple of hours later before tennis. Aspirin came after tennis and before back-to-school shopping, before dinner, and before bed.

When I complained, my mother said, "You'll get over it once school and sports start."

A week later, I struggled out of bed and trudged off to school. If anything, the pain was worse. At volleyball tryouts, I was sidelined before I finished the first warm-up lap around the quarter-mile track. Four days later, I stopped at the foot of a flight of stairs at school and shifted my books to use the handrail. The friend I'd been walking with, a girl who'd easily made the volleyball team with her powerful legs and accurate sets, was a few steps up before she turned to find me still at the bottom. "You are so slow these days," she said. "What is with you?"

Groups of students brushed past me. The look on my face—maybe it was confusion or fear or pain or a combination of the three—brought my friend to my side. Tears ran down my cheeks. "I can't even get up the first step I'm in so much pain. You've got to get me to the nurse's office."

At home, my mother immediately called our doctor. He told her to put me to bed, continue to give me aspirin, and give me a good soak in a hot tub. He was sure I would feel better the next day.

Wrong! Friday dawned, and the pain had spread through every sinew and made movement impossible. Dr. Hilsman rushed to our house. After careful examination, he turned to my mother. "I'm sure she has polio," he said. "Normally, we'd do a spinal tap to confirm, but the hospital's in the middle of a major remodel, and she'd end up in a hallway." He ran a hand over his close-cut red hair. "I'm sure it's polio. I'll call the Warm Springs Polio Foundation and get them to see her. It's only a hundred miles from here. You can manage the trip up and back in a day."

It didn't occur to me that this was anything serious, so I wasn't particularly worried. The following day, my parents and I arrived at the foundation hospital. An orderly lifted me from the car to a stretcher and wheeled me into an examining room. As I lay on the table, a doctor with cold, damp hands lifted my hand. "Move your thumb," he said. Nothing. "How about your leg?" Again, not a twitch.

My father's tall thin frame rested against the door jam. Every few minutes he rotated his wrist to sneak a peek at his watch. My mother stood a little closer, but back, in order to give the doctor room. Her hands clasped and unclasped while her eyes centered on me.

My father must have checked his watch fifteen times in twice as many minutes. The only sounds during all this time were the doctor's noisy breathing and the crinkle of white paper under me as he poked and prodded. When he finally spoke, it was to my parents. "I have no idea what this is, but I can tell you it's not polio. We'll need to run a series of tests. I want to start this afternoon."

The four hours of testing caused pain beyond any I'd experienced up to that point. It felt as though my muscles were being shot through with millions of high-voltage needles. By the time the tests stopped, my relief was so great that I didn't particularly care what the results were. I just wanted my father to carry me to our car's sun-warmed back seat, tuck me in safely, and drive us all home.

Back in the exam room with my parents, the doctor (Bennett he'd told me during my torture session) said, "The results look like nothing we've ever seen before. It could be muscular dystrophy, but it is going to take more tests."

More tests? If I could have, I would have run and kept running until I was as far away as possible from Dr. Bennett. The opposite end of the earth couldn't be too far. Those steps at school? No problem. Just let me at 'em one more time. I'll do them and the next flight, too. Dr. Bennett's voice interrupted my thoughts of a two-steps-at-a-time bound up those stairs. "We'll need to keep her here at the hospital for about thirty days."

Did he say thirty days? Here? I couldn't imagine another thirty minutes! "Can't you just give me a prescription or a shot?" I'd never been in a hospital except to have my tonsils out, and the thought, especially given my introduction via "testing," was terrifying. "Will my parents be able to stay with me?"

The clammy hand landed on my bare shoulder and squeezed. "No. The tests will take up most of your time. They wouldn't be able to see you during the day."

"Panic" is not a strong enough word, and "terror" is too reminiscent of an Alfred Hitchcock movie, but what I felt was something between the two. Something razor sharp sailing too close, too fast. In your dreams, it is the thing you know you can't outrun, the thing that paralyzes you.

My mother stroked my head, blue eyes fixed on mine. Her always perfectly coifed hair was slightly ruffled. "We want you to get well, Lynne. Daddy needs to be at work, and I need to be home with your sisters and–" she hesitated. Her gaze flicked to my father and then back. "This is the best place for you."

My parents walked on either side of my stretcher as a tall orderly, thin as drainpipe, wheeled me down the hall and into a room occupied by a girl who couldn't have been more than nine. I kept up a brave face while my parents and I said our good-byes, but as soon as the nurse swept them from the room, panic ping-ponged through me. My mind railed against the plain walls washed in a pale green, the window too far away to see out of, the steel frame around my bed that turned it into a crib, and the nine-year-old in the other bed. Tears hung on the rims of my eyes, but I was determined not to cry. Held back, my tears took the form of a quivering that started in my chin and then took hold in my shoulders.

The nine-year-old turned to me, the freckles on the bridge of her nose pale against her paler skin. "It's okay to cry," she said in a voice both quiet and kind. "I cried, too, when my parents left."

The next morning, an aide sporting a nest of curly black hair bustled in with my breakfast tray. "Time to eat," she said. "I've been assigned to feed you." She said this in a matter-of-fact way, as if it were the most normal thing in the world to be feeding someone over the age of two. She shoveled food into my mouth at an incredible speed. I said, "Please don't feed me so fast. I can't eat that fast."

The aide continued on with her methodic spooning. She wasn't doing it right. "Stop it!" I said and clamped my mouth shut against the spoonful of scrambled eggs. The spoon halted. "I don't want to eat with someone else feeding me. I don't want the eggs and then the bacon. I want the bacon and then the eggs."

She met my eyes. No anger or judgment, just her sizing me up before she turned the spoon and offered me the handle. My mind told my arm to lift and my fingers to close around the spoon and guide it to my mouth, but all I could do was stare. My arms wouldn't move.

Day in and day out, I underwent a battery of tests and saw

doctor after doctor after doctor. At long last, my parents returned, and we all met with Dr. Bennett. "We still have no idea what this disease is," he said. "But we're going to consult with doctors at the Mayo Clinic and Emory University Medical School. Hopefully, they can shed some new light. Meanwhile, Lynne needs to stay here. She wouldn't be able to function at home."

In addition to all of the medical tests, I had to have physical therapy several times a day to keep my muscles from shriveling. The doctors explained that if the muscles weren't stretched, my legs and arms would draw up against my body and atrophy. If they didn't put me in a standing position, strapped to a special "standing table," at least once a day, my kidneys would fail. The pain during all of this was the same excruciating pain I'd endured during those first four hours of testing. I learned very quickly to take my mind outside my body and think of something, anything, that would distract me.

Weeks turned into months. At the end of six months, I was no better. If anything, I was worse. My weight dropped to eighty-five pounds, and I was skeleton thin. I was in tremendous pain. I couldn't sit up by myself and had to be strapped into the wheelchair so I wouldn't flop out. My eyes were so weak they couldn't hold a focus and crossed if I tried to read. Teenagers are supposed to be fixing their hair and experimenting with makeup. They're supposed to make themselves look pretty. They aren't supposed to look like skeletons, be strapped into wheelchairs, and wear thick, ugly glasses because of crossed eyes.

Finally, after eight months, the doctors had a diagnosis: polymyositis, an inflammation of the muscle fibers. My parents were told I wouldn't survive, and I was told I'd never walk again. The doctor explained that my medical team was looking at the latest advances in hopes of finding a way to treat me, but he made it clear that my chances of survival were slim; if I did survive, I might be able to use my arms but not my legs.

I couldn't believe what I was hearing; I couldn't believe that the doctor of all people was giving up on me. I turned my head toward Dr. Bennett, pinned him from behind my thick lenses, and said, "Listen here. I have no intention of dying or of spending the rest of my life in a wheel chair. It makes no difference what you say, and I don't care how long it takes. I know I will live, and I know I will walk again."

I spent a total of two years in the hospital while I fought for my life, and the next four years learning how to walk again. After the first year, a miracle occurred. The pharmaceutical company, for whom my father worked, developed a new, revolutionary anti-inflammatory drug. It was in clinical trials and, with the permission of Dr. Bennett and the Food and Drug Administration; I was put into an experimental program. Every day, I took the medication and a physical therapist put a strap around my waist and dangled me like a puppet. He would put his foot behind mine, push one leg forward and then the other. At the end of twelve months, I suddenly pushed my foot forward by myself. Inch by inch and day by day, during the next four years, I walked back into life, away from a disease that had been reported only forty-eight times in medical history, a disease claiming zero survivors. I was the first.

By the time I was in my mid-forties, the years spent in the hospital were only a distant memory. I had a flourishing career, a loving marriage, and two wonderful children who were considered late-in-life babies-one born when I was thirty-seven and the other when I was forty.

I was earning money I had only imagined and had been promoted to a position as director of international sales and marketing for a division of a large billion-dollar corporation. I received many awards for management and excellence in marketing. I traveled two weeks a month and stopped off in more than thirty different countries. I considered myself to be a very important person.

Suddenly, cancer collided with this demanding career, and I woke up to realize that I hardly knew my children and hardly knew what life outside the office was like. The ninety-hour work week and images of great success filled my mind. Cancer stepped in and taught me I was missing the point.

Terminal illnesses have a startling way of forcing people to face the truths in their lives—truths I did not face at sixteen but that I encountered head on with cancer. This book is about my journey through cancer–a journey that is filled with tears, anger, fear, surprise, and joy. While my body underwent major changes, my soul and spirit started to thrive.

I have found balance in life by juggling work, play, family, friends, and even strangers who need comfort. This is a long cry from the busy jet-setting executive who was too busy and too important, so she thought, to take time for others.

This book reveals my innermost thoughts and feelings throughout the process of cancer. It is in these words that I pour out my soul, my fears, and my confusion. Through these words, I begin the process of slowly awakening into a new being.

One evening, I had the opportunity to hear Dr. Depak Chopra speak. A comment he made rang through my head for many days: "The space between our thoughts is the window to our soul." When I heard this, I realized that before cancer, I had no space between my thoughts. I allowed no idle moments in my busy schedule. The window to my soul was boarded up.

Cancer forced that window to open. For days following each chemotherapy treatment, my brain seemed filled with cotton, and thoughts eluded me. It was during this time that my emotions spilled out onto my computer keyboard. It was then that I allowed myself to peek through the window. As you read this book, know that you are looking directly into my soul.

Chapter Two

*While my body underwent major changes,
my soul and spirit started to thrive.*

I t has been three years since my last mammogram. I have been so busy with my career that I hardly notice the time lapse. Every time someone talks about breast cancer and the need for a mammogram, I put on my halo and speak eloquently about how I always have mine on time. Women who are afraid to get them are silly. The postcard reminder arrived about eight or nine months ago, at the two-year mark. I made a mental note to schedule an appointment on my next pass through town.

Four more months zip by. During this time, my seventy-five-year-old mother-in-law discovers she has breast cancer. It is very far advanced, and I preach to my husband about how foolish she was to have never had a mammogram. I certainly always have mine. That reminds me, I need to make that appointment the next time I'm in town.

Over the next three months, my mother-in-law's cancer progresses rapidly. My career grows almost as fast. Flying around the world and doing business in countries from Japan to Russia to Cyprus are parts of my regular routine. Jet lag never affects me. I am almost as proud of my ability to travel from time zone to time zone, on two to three hours of sleep, as I am about my "regular" physicals and mammograms.

In between my trips every two or three weeks, my time is spent running between soccer games, Girl Scouts, football, homework, violin lessons, and on and on. Endless activities consume every moment of my spare time. My husband has more than an hour-long commute to his job, and, being raised in the era where "the mother does it all," I am very proud of my ability to do it all. I really believe I am invincible and that family and work demands simply do not permit me to slow down long enough to think about my own health.

As I whiz through an airport on yet another international journey, six months after my fiftieth birthday, the book *Silent Passage* by Gail Sheehy[1] catches my eye in the corner bookstand. Hmmm. I have a long flight ahead, and because I just turned fifty, maybe I had better begin to prepare myself for menopause. So I grab the book and begin reading on the plane.

Not long into it, she speaks of the need for women over fifty to have regular breast exams by a physician and, between those, regular self-exams. I have been told that cancer caught in the early stages is highly treatable, and yet I have never gotten around to scheduling that two-year mammogram. It's probably academic anyway. I'll do it as soon as I get home, but tonight, at the very least, I'll do the self-exam she describes in her book.

As I lie in my bed and read the instructions, with the book in one hand and the other doing the exam, my left breast feels hard–like a rock. Why is it is so hard? I'm looking for a lump–something small and round and hard, like a pea. This isn't little. This doesn't feel like a pea. This just feels like the top half of my left breast is solid. Weird.

I sit up and reread the symptoms in the book, symptoms I have read many, many times before. It doesn't say anything about the entire breast feeling hard, but the sign that pops goose bumps over my arms and legs is "puckered nipple."

Good grief. My nipple looks like it has a small pucker in the top edge. In the bathroom, the hotel mirror reveals the pucker clearly. A shiver runs down my spine. No matter which way I turn, I still see it there.

Most of the night and early morning, I poke and squeeze my breast from every angle possible, fully expecting to be black and blue by sunrise. An early morning alarm catapults me from the bed to the bathroom mirror. Maybe last night's panic was a combination of bad light and an overly active imagination. But no, the pucker's still there along with puffy eyes, the whites road-mapped in red. As I brush my teeth, I stare at my breast. Is this real? Is it my imagination? I would feel so stupid running to my doctor in a panic only to find out nothing is wrong with me. Somehow I think I have to have a temperature of one hundred and five to justify a visit. Will he laugh at me? Will he scold me for not getting my mammogram on time?

I can't afford to let conjecture about a lump and a pucker rattle my presentation at the sales meeting I'm leading. Anyway, I'm in Sweden, many time zones from home, so it will be hours before I can call for an appointment with my gynecologist. I'll have to make some excuse to weasel out of the meeting, which is definitely not my style. I'm always annoyed with people who disrupt a meeting's flow to attend to personal business. What's even more irritating is that this could have been avoided altogether if I'd just sandwiched a mammogram between business trips.

During my presentation, the havoc in my mind reveals itself on the faces of my colleagues clustered at the back of the room. Their expressions are a mix of puzzlement and apprehension as they witness the difference between this presentation and the last. One minute my presentation is solid, unfolding like the one before it. The next minute I catch myself wondering when I'll be able to get to a phone and schedule an appointment with my gynecologist. Then, I stumble on material I know by heart. The day is a continuous struggle to maintain equilibrium. I feel schizophrenic.

Finally, it is morning in Oregon. I call for a break in the seminar and rush to the nearest phone. Oh, please, let them answer and not put me on hold. I have only a ten-minute window. I can't keep interrupting the seminar with breaks. A live person answers the phone. I'm prepared for the usual wait of three to four weeks for an appointment, but following a brief description of the symptoms, the receptionist says, "Come in this afternoon." I explain that I am out of the country and the earliest I can come in is the following Tuesday. She schedules me for 10 a.m. What happened to the doctor's busy schedule? Usually, all I hear is, "Sorry, he will not be able to see you for three weeks or three months." Next Tuesday? That fast? I've never gotten an appointment this quickly.

For the next week, I am obsessed with my breast. I poke and squeeze it constantly and stare at it every time I'm near a mirror. I carry out my exams whenever fear runs down my spine. It doesn't matter if I'm on an airplane, walking through an airport, or checking out of a hotel.

I am surprised I am not arrested for lewd behavior. There is no telling where or when I carry out my exam.

I fly home on the weekend and impatiently wait for the appointment, all the time continuing to check my breast. The closer to the appointment, the more I squeeze and push in hopes that the "rock" will disappear before Tuesday. I vacillate between telling myself it is nothing and being convinced I am going to die any minute. The next five days pass at a snail's pace.

Repeatedly, I tell myself that this is absolutely nothing. I'm just being paranoid. When I go to the doctor, he's going to tell me I'm exaggerating. I come close to calling and canceling the appointment. Several of my friends have had breast lumps and bumps over the years, and they're all fine. I expect the same result even though that puckered nipple persists.

Tuesday finally arrives, and I, who normally fly into the doctor's office five minutes late while proclaiming how I couldn't get away from the office, burst in five minutes early. In the waiting room, I fidget in a shallow-seated, sea foam-colored chair, the kind of chair built not for comfort but for marking time. I sneak glances at the other patients: a woman dressed as I am, for business. The speed with which she flips through the pages of glossy women's magazine shows this is just a detour from the purpose of her day. Her mind is probably three hours down the road as she mentally ticks through her to-do list.

I check my watch, work backward from my noon lunch meeting, resist the urge to ask the receptionist how late the doctor's running, tap the toe of my pump on the plush carpet, and don't even get the satisfaction of the attendant tap tap tap. My eyes close, and a deep breath follows and takes the edge off. The doctor is not in any hurry.

This will take as long as it takes. Another deep breath and I imagine I hear his familiar voice reassuring me as it has through the birth of my children and a gazillion minor ailments and the routine exams of the past twenty years. I imagine him speaking, "This is nothing, Lynne! But we had better check just to make sure. We'll just run a few routine tests." By the time the nurse interrupts my reverie, I've talked myself into believing this visit is a complete waste of time.

After the usual catch-up on kids and golf, Dr. Schrinsky begins his exam. The exam is silent—long and silent. I follow his eyes, the way his brush, stiff eyebrows come together above the wide bridge of his nose as his hands palpate the rock in my left breast over and over. I am not hearing any reassurances. When he speaks, it's only to say, "Turn around. Now put your hands together. Squeeze. Lie down. Sit up. Raise your arms." Aside from these orders, his silence is absolute. Why isn't he telling me this is nothing?

When the exam is over, Dr. Schrinsky finally speaks. "In your last mammogram, there was a spot on your right breast. The report says it was a calcium deposit. It didn't show anything in your left breast, the one we're looking at today. So I don't think there is a connection between the two, but I can't be sure. I'm going to have the lab reread it, but in the meantime, we have to get a new mammogram."

I hear only caution, not reassurance, not hope. My mind resembles a kite string ripped by the wind. It is unspooling at a rate too fast to control.

The doctor eases onto a stool across from me. He alternates between glances at me and the file in his lap. He is very contemplative. "Lynne, we can spend all day debating the characteristics of benign versus malignant breast lumps," he says, "but this one has a lot of characteristics of a malignancy. You need to have a mammogram today or tomorrow at the latest."

His almost fatherly concern grates, and I get defensive. "I'm really busy right now. I have to go to Canada tomorrow. Surely one more day won't matter." I start in on the long list of trips and tasks scheduled for my "very important" job. Maybe if I have enough excuses and he understands how inconvenient all of this is, it will go away. Through him, God will say, "Okay, I know you didn't mean to neglect your body and forget your check-ups. You've learned your lesson. Now keep better tabs on your health."

My wild imagining is interrupted by his hesitant words. "Last time you were in, we talked about jet lag and the affect all this traveling could have on your body. I honestly think this constant traveling has affected your health and weakened your immune system. I'll let it go one more day, but when you get back, run, don't walk, to your mammogram."

My mind whirls. How dare you! I don't get jet lag. I feel just fine. In some twisted form of logic, I think if I get angry enough, maybe this will go away. Maybe he will change his mind. I fully expect God to change his mind; my doctor can do the same.

After listening to my excuses and ramblings about how important my work is, he sits quietly for a few moments, studies his shoes, and then says, "Let's see what the tests show." As he turns to leave, his silence blasts in my ears.

For a few more minutes, I sit on the cold exam table and try to digest what's happening. A familiar voice in my head says, "Good grief, this is absolutely nothing. This is all just an exercise in caution. Last year, my friend Cathy went through the same thing. The doctors took three weeks to get around to doing all her tests, and it turned out to be nothing at all. I'm sure this is the same thing."

As I head out to the reception area, the nurse says, "Good luck." Good luck? Why is she saying "Good luck"? Does she think there is something seriously wrong? A moment of panic comes over me, and then just as quickly, my confidence returns, and with a casual smile and a quick "thanks," I stroll out of the office.

Wednesday, I put this whole thing out of my mind, head to Canada, and carry on quite normally. I'm really good at focusing only on the tasks at hand. My motto is a standard joke in our family: I'm only moving clouds today; tomorrow, I'll move mountains.

Thursday arrives, and I get the mammogram as scheduled. Assuming it will take a day or two to hear the results, I head to my office and become enmeshed in work. Within hours, my doctor calls.

"Lynne, your mammogram doesn't show a distinct malignancy, but it does show a change in the architecture of your breast. The radiologist isn't sure what it means, but he thinks it's serious enough that you need a biopsy. I'm going to arrange for you to see a surgeon on Monday."

"What? I'm supposed to go to Bangkok next Thursday for a sales meeting. I have distributors coming in from ten different countries. It's all scheduled. Can't I postpone the biopsy until I get back?" Dead silence. I try again, "Okay, what if I just put off my trip until after the biopsy? Once the biopsy is done, I'll need to wait for the results, anyway. No sense sitting around at home and worrying." I'm so busy mentally justifying my position that it takes me a while to notice the silence on the other end of the line. Then, the words sink into my heart, and I know my fate as he quietly says, "Lynne, cancel your trip. You're not going anywhere."

Not going anywhere? How wrong he is. Fasten your seat belt. This journey is just beginning.

Chapter Three

I know now that nothing about me
or my life will be the same again.

The sales meeting in Bangkok is for my largest distributors who will be flying in from Korea, Japan, Australia, Indonesia, and the rest of the Pacific Rim countries. It is supposed to be a great meeting–at long last, the launching of the new product guaranteed to propel the company into a major player in the worldwide market. I have been frantically trying to catch up on work for this meeting, but my ears continue to ring with Dr. Schrinsky's warning to cancel my trip. I shake it off by telling myself that these things are always nothing. Everyone gets all excited, and then it ends up being nothing. It has been like a whirlwind getting ready for the meeting, and I haven't seen much of my family. After this trip, I plan on spending a little time at home.

It's always difficult telling my children, Keaton and Dana, that I can't go to their school plays or sporting events, but I'm good at rationalization. They're still young, eleven and fourteen. I have many years to spend time with them. I do spend a lot of time with them. When I'm in town, I take them to the zoo, their games, their music lessons, and I always have birthday parties for them–even if the party is a week later than the actual birthday.

But the thought "You may have cancer" keeps ringing in my head. Good grief, I don't have time for these kinds of thoughts.

Compartmentalize this, Lynne. Close the worry compartment, and focus on this meeting. It is a simple case of mind over matter. My hectic work pace continues, every moment filled, and when there's a lull, I start in on the minutia my assistant could easily handle. At lunch, I dash out to the bank and decide to grab a meal at the first fast food place I can find. Hamburger and fries. Eating on the run seems to be the norm these days. I work late into the night and prepare for the Bangkok meeting. Today, this is all I am focusing on, nothing else.

Friday morning, I'm at my desk early to organize my mind before the inevitable flood of phone calls that ensues before an international meeting. I haven't said anything to anyone about my doctor visits or having tests: not my husband, not my boss, and certainly not my children. I see no point in setting off alarms when I am convinced it is going to be an academic exercise.

Today, I have a last-minute meeting with the development engineers before shipping the demo product to Bangkok, and as predicted, the phone rings constantly. By late morning, I'm irritated at yet another interruption. I grab the phone and intend to hang up quickly so I can get to my meeting on time.

"Hello, Lynne? It's Dr. Schrinsky. I've just made arrangements for Dr. Holmes, the surgeon, to see you on Monday. His schedule is very busy, and I asked him to squeeze you in. He wants you to call his office and set up the appointment."

"Do I really have to disrupt his schedule? It doesn't sound very convenient for him, and because I'll only be gone a week, I promise I'll see him as soon as I get back." Schrinsky gives the loudest silence I have ever heard. It is deafening and seems to last forever. After a long pause, he speaks quietly, "No, Lynne. This can't wait. You need to be there Monday. They're waiting for your call."

The busy receptionist at Dr. Holmes's office tells me I can't get an appointment for two weeks! Irritated, I tell her Dr. Holmes has already agreed to see me Monday. "Just a minute, I'll check." As I sit on hold, my irritation mounts. Two weeks? I am going to cancel my trip and then not be able to see him for two weeks? Soon, she is back on the line. "Lynne, he'll see you Monday at 11:30."

My world begins to crash around me. This just will not go away. Why me? Who is this person I'm seeing on Monday? I stare out the window and let the tears stream down my cheeks. I've been so busy raising the kids, traveling here and there, trying to keep up with my work and family. Somehow, the mammogram just kept slipping my mind. It wasn't that I didn't want to get one; I just forgot to call until I was sitting on an airplane or was in some distant place where I couldn't get to a phone. It never crossed my mind that something might be wrong. I assumed I would know intuitively if I had a serious disease.

The books don't tell you that breast cancer doesn't always have symptoms: coughs, upset stomach, pain, something. I don't even have a lump, just a hard breast. Maybe it will turn out to be nothing. Maybe Dr. Schrinsky is just being overly cautious.

The blaring intercom snaps me out of my stupor. "Lynne Massie, the meeting has started." What was so critical five minutes ago has become insignificant. Tears stain the back of my sleeve. In a fog, I gather my things, walk into the conference room, and say, "I'm sorry. Something very important has come up, and I can't be here for the meeting." The entire staff is speechless. Without further explanation, I simply leave and head for home. I want to prepare a beautiful dinner for my family. No frozen dinners tonight. Mom has found time to cook.

As I leave the office, tears come to my eyes while I fumble with my car keys. What if there is something seriously wrong? On my way home, I force myself to put away my tears. I am on my way to pick up my kids at their after-school program, and I don't want them to see me crying. They are surprised at how early I arrive and are thrilled when I mention making pizza for dinner. They run ahead to the car, brown heads bobbing at the same height even though Dana is three years older than Keaton. "Tiny but mighty" is how she describes herself, and I have to agree. She takes the word "no" as a challenge, not a discouragement.

A few years back, I'd been saying no about getting a second dog for some time. Then, one rainy Saturday afternoon, Dana asked whether we could just visit the Humane Society. "No, Dana, we are not getting another dog. One is enough." Dana assured me we were only looking, and looking is what we did until we were met with a very sad pair of eyes peering through a wire cage. "Ohhhh, Mom, look at this."

"Dana, we're here to look, remember?" The sad eyes belonged to a very large police dog, skinny with stiff brown and black hair and big ears. One of the volunteers working that day, a fresh-faced young woman with her straight blonde hair pulled back in an elastic, stopped and slid her fingers through the Shepherd's cage. The dog gently licked at her hand. So delicate for such a big dog. "Sheba's a sweetie," the young woman said. "Spent her first three or four years with a family that neglected and abused her. They left her tied to a tree when they skipped town in the middle of the night."

This wasn't some ordinary dog. Those eyes pleaded for love. How could a dog that has every reason to hate human beings be so gentle and kind? So sweet and caring? The young woman told us no one had even considered Sheba for adoption. "Of course not," I said. "She's waiting for us."

That was two years ago, and Sheba is firmly entrenched as a valuable member of the family. Dana is now fourteen and Keaton eleven. Keaton is chubby, big compared to his classmates, and a bit of a worrier. He is not the kind of child to shrug things off. When he was little, he watched the space shuttle Challenger explode on television. The explosion and subsequent deaths of the crew made such an impact that from then on, Keaton was convinced my business flights would meet with the same fate, no matter how many times Hal and I explained that space ships were very different from airplanes.

The pizza is a big hit, and now we move through the weekend, which is agony. My husband, Hal, is overseas on a business trip, and I try to behave as calmly as possible. When I think the kids aren't looking, tears run down my face. I am really having trouble hiding my fear. On Saturday evening, I spy the kids playing with Sheba and Snookers, our white Samoyed, in the family room while I cook. The picture is so Norman Rockwell: two brown-haired, brown-eyed kids, wrestling with their dogs while waiting for supper. The image, the potential disruption of it, hits me hard. What's going to happen to all of us? The next moment, Keaton catches my glance. I work up a smile for him but can tell by the wrinkle on his brow that he's not buying it. I need to pull myself together. After all, I have no clear information. Maybe the doctors are going to tell me I'm fine, and all this worry will be for naught.

When Hal calls over the weekend, I say casually that I have had a mammogram that week. I say nothing else. I don't want to alarm him over the phone or discuss this without some concrete information. I especially don't want to take a chance on the kids overhearing. But in bed at night, I cry to God, "What are you doing to me? How can you let this happen? Is this just a scare to make me slow down?" God's silence is as thick as Dr. Schrinsky's.

Sunday morning before service at church, the minister wanders among the congregation and chats. She touches my shoulder and asks how I am. Suddenly, I am one ragged breath away from losing control. I've been coming to this church for only three months and, not knowing her very well, don't want her to think I'm a complete idiot. I put on my business demeanor and in a very matter-of-fact manner say, "A little tense. I had a mammogram on Thursday and have to see a surgeon tomorrow. I don't know everything that is going on, and I'm sure everything is just fine. But do you think maybe you could say a small prayer for me? I'm not sure about God at this point, so my prayers are more like screaming."

On Monday morning, I get the kids off to school and do a very good job of hiding the fear bound up in my wobbly legs. At the surgeon's office, my fingers tap the chair as I read and reread the same page in an out-of-date magazine. After what seems like an eternity, the nurse comes out. "It's your turn, Lynne."

The exam room has the usual trappings: exam table, chair on wheels, little sink. Opposite the door is a big window that overlooks the Willamette River. The day is sunny, rare in Portland. On the far side of the river is a wooded ridge still untouched by the expanding suburbs. The beautiful scenery sets off an ache in my heart. I spend so little time enjoying the view. One of these days, I'm going to see it from the ground up rather than from 35,000 feet looking down.

I undress as if I am a robot moving in slow motion. Reluctant to pull down the zippers and undo the buttons, I feel that each step toward nakedness is taking me closer to some unknown fate. Once in the skimpy gown, I sit on the table with the cold draft on my back, and I wait. The world is bright and sunny. Life is good. I have a lump. Not a big lump. A small lump, but a lump.

Dr. Holmes is an older gentleman, white hair and half-glasses. The exam goes on in silence for ten minutes before he says, "Sit up. Squeeze your hands together. Turn sideways. Lie down." And so it goes for what seems like an eternity. During the arm and hand squeezing, my focus keeps shifting from inside the room to the serene view.

Finally, Dr. Holmes peers over his half-glasses and says, "You have cancer." The view remains exactly as it was only moments before.

My eyes find their way back from the view and meet his eyes behind the half-glasses. "What?"

"You have cancer."

It can't be. You only have to look at the view to know the world is okay. I'm okay. I have to be. "But I feel fine. Don't people feel something when they have cancer? I have no pain, no discomfort, no sickness. It has to be a mistake."

My life is disintegrating with each passing second. I swallow hard, fighting the lump in my stomach, the hysteria. Surely they can't diagnose cancer on the spot. This man has glanced at my x-rays and given me a ten-minute exam. He looks me straight in the eye and says, "This is Monday. I want to do a biopsy on Thursday. Between now and then, we have to determine how extensive this is and how far it may have spread."

For some stupid reason, I actually think he is joking. When I look at him for confirmation, he asks in a serious tone, "Do you have headaches? There's a good chance this has spread to your brain or your lungs. It could also be in your liver and bones. Do you have any pain when I push down on your ribs?"

It is taking all I have to sit here and keep breathing. My mind reels between a silent scream and the doctor's litany of tests. The biopsy, it turns out, is only a small cog in a big wheel. Blood tests, brain scans, bone scans, liver scans, x-rays, and on and on. Three days of tests. I want him to say I'm going to be just fine. Instead, he says, "This tumor's quite large. At the very least, you're going to have to have a mastectomy. The whole breast has to go. This is too big for a lumpectomy, and radiation is out of the question. Prepare yourself for chemotherapy."

Dumbfounded, his words hit me scattershot.

"Realize the purpose of the biopsy isn't to determine whether this is malignant. It is. What we're going to do is determine the type of cancer you have and its aggressiveness."

His benevolent manner does little to soften the blow. My tears blur his face and the view. "Will I live?" I ask with the expectation of a child. I fully expect him to say I'll be fine. Instead, he says, "The survival rate for women with small tumors is quite high, but I think you've probably had this for at least two years, and more than likely, the tumor has spread."

He lifts his glasses and massages the indents on his nose. "I'm really sorry to have to be the bearer of bad news." He pats my shoulder on his way out. "I'll see you at the hospital Thursday for the biopsy. Meanwhile, Deloris will set up the rest of the tests and let you know the schedule."

My eyes shift to the window. I am flabbergasted at the news and the barrage of assaults on my body that are scheduled for the next four days. I came here expecting to hear something positive, and this complete stranger is telling me the worst news imaginable.

"Excuse me," I blurt out, "but before you go, I have a few questions. I just met you thirty minutes ago. I have no idea who you are, and now you're asking me to put my life in your hands. For all I know, you take off warts for a living and decided that it might be fun to do breasts now and then. 'Hmmm. I think I'll remove breasts instead of warts. Much more glamorous, you know. Certainly more money.' I trust Dr. Schrinsky, so I guess I'm supposed to trust you, but I really would like to know what qualifies you to save my life."

Stunned, he stares at me. Then, after a few seconds, he smiles and lets out a small chuckle. "Fair question. I'm a cancer survivor. My wife is an oncology nurse. Fifty percent of my patients have cancer, the majority of them breast cancer. I deal with this every day, every week.

Lynne, believe me, I want you to live as much as you want to live."

I let out a big sigh. "I suppose any doctor can do tests. I don't see any risk there, but I don't know how good you are. Somewhere out there is a doctor who graduated last in his class from the worst school in the country, and somewhere out there is a doctor who graduated top in his class from the best school. I have no idea where you fit on the scale. We'll go ahead with the tests, but before we go any further, I intend to check you out." He peers at me over his half-glasses, chuckles again, and says, "That's a deal."

Still in a state of shock, my eyes dart back to the view–the sun strong and sure in a sky of storybook blue, the Willamette River secure in its wide banks, and the wooded ridge beyond untouched. The contrast between the view and what I'm hearing sets off a whirlwind in my mind. My life has changed in a breath, yet the view remains the same. Thursday. Three more days. It begins Thursday. The view won't change. I will change. I will lose my breast. I will lose my hair. I will lose my way of life. I could lose my life. How can this be? The window frames one world, the door to this office another. How can so much change in such a short time and yet so much remain the same?

Deloris the nurse comes in, takes one look at my red eyes, and hands me a box of tissues. Patting me on the shoulder, she says, "Did anyone come with you this morning?"

"No," I manage to choke out. "My husband's out of town. I didn't believe this was anything serious, so I didn't think to have someone come along."

She looks at me like a grandmother. "Take your time to digest this. Go ahead and cry. We don't need the room until you're through." The door shuts behind her with a soft click.

And so I sit feeling despair, sadness, disbelief. I know now that nothing about me or my life will ever be the same again. I look at the view. I hear his words. My world is crashing down around me. The view has betrayed me. It will stay constant as it has for all these years. I will not. Nothing about me or my life will ever be the same again. I am instantly different.

Chapter Four

"Mom, is cancer worse than the flu?"

I gather my things, grab some extra tissues, and head for my car in a daze. Hunkered behind the steering wheel in the doctor's parking lot, I know I am beginning a journey I don't want to be on. I see nothing positive in this and am convinced God has it in for me.

I have no idea what to do. Part of me is in complete denial. I'm supposed to have cancer, yet I feel fine, fine enough to go back to my office, work the rest of the day, and fix supper for my family—fine enough to blithely carry on as if none of this is happening. Another part of me desperately needs to talk with someone, anyone. This part of me is a terrified three-year-old lost in the park. She knows nothing about being an executive in control.

Driving takes great effort, although the effort is automatic. It's almost surreal the way my hands and feet go through the motions while my brain alternately races and idles. I'm not even sure where I'm going. Streets I've known for years look oddly unfamiliar, as if I'm seeing them for the first time. Was that sign always there, that park bench?

The sign of the local mini-mart catches my eye. Thirst. I'm thirsty. The car wheels into the lot and somehow stops in front of the glass double doors. In a daze, I push through one of the doors. It's heavy and saps my strength enough that I wonder whether I'll be able to drive home. The young clerk looks up, snaps her gum, and, in a cheery voice says, "Good morning. Isn't this a great day?"

The comment snaps me out of my fog. She has got to be kidding. This is the worst day of my life! Does she have any idea what I was just told? I muster up all my strength and use great restraint not to shout out, "I have cancer! Would you want someone asking whether you're having a good day? Don't be stupid."

Instead, I smile, acknowledge her remark, and thank her for her good wishes. In return, I give my good wishes. I am amazed that I can be two completely different people in a single moment: happy and cheerful, telling her to have a good day, while the three-year-old in my head is screaming, "How dare you!"

I pay for the drink and return to my car. I want to call Hal. He is an engineer, in Taiwan on business. Other than telling him I had the mammogram, I didn't say much about this to him over the weekend when he called—mostly because I didn't want the kids to overhear me and I didn't want to worry him unnecessarily. Also, a big part of me was still denying anything could be seriously wrong.

Checking my watch, I mentally click into the time differences and figure it's Monday here, so it is around 3 a.m. Tuesday in the Pacific Rim. It isn't really fair to wake him up. At least I've had a little time in the light of day to absorb the news, but I am desperate to talk with him. For this, he can wake up. From my car phone in the convenience store parking lot, I dial his hotel. "Hal, I'm sorry to wake you, but, I have some really bad news. No, the kids are fine. It's me."

"Two weeks ago, in Sweden, I found a—not really a lump in my breast—but sort of like a lump," I say. "My breast was really hard. I told you I had a mammogram, but what I didn't tell you was that I got a call from Dr. Schrinsky. He said it didn't look good, so he sent me to a surgeon this morning. The surgeon took one look at my x-rays and told me I have breast cancer."

Groggily, he mumbles, "What?"

The steering wheel goes blurry behind my tears. "Hal, is there any way you can call your boss and tell him you're coming home? The surgeon hasn't done any tests yet. They're going to do them all this week. But he examined me, looked at my x-rays, and diagnosed me on the spot. The biopsy's Thursday. Do you think you can be home by then?" He assures me, "Absolutely. I'll call the travel agent right away." Once Hal hangs up, my thoughts turn to my mother. How many times have I called her in tears? How many times, when I was just out of college, did I call to cry on her shoulder because I had a broken heart or something went wrong at work?

That was twenty-five years ago. My mother is now much older and is a constant worrywart. She is four thousand miles away, and I just don't think I can cope with her arriving on the next plane. I need time alone with Hal and the kids. I need time to gather my thoughts. This is so sudden I feel like a robot going through the motions of looking and functioning normally.

A pile of soppy tissues is building on the passenger side floor. I think of my friends who are all at work. I can't call them yet. I want to talk to someone, and I don't want to talk to someone. Besides, it is the middle of the day, and I don't want to interrupt their workday with my bad news. So I sit in my car as if in a trance. Maybe I'll just go back to work and try to get my mind on something else. But I don't want to tell the people at work just now either. It is too soon. I am supposed to be the leader of this major project. I am supposed to be going to Bangkok this week! They will want answers right away about what is going to happen, and I don't have any answers. No, I can't deal with that right now. I'll get it taken care of in time to cover the Bangkok meeting. The company will survive. I may not.

My thoughts turn to Victoria, the minister at the Unity World Healing Center. Instantly, I think of her as my minister. The Unity church is a far cry from the staunch Episcopal church where I grew up and had my children baptized. For years, I sang in the choir. My children went to Sunday school. Then, my life got very busy, and I began traveling. My favorite minister left, and that particular church stopped feeding my soul. On the rare Sundays I found myself home, I simply stopped getting up to go.

I discovered Unity when my friend Lee introduced me to A Course in Miracles[2]. Philosophically, the metaphysical beliefs seemed to mesh with the person I had become. Yesterday at the Unity church, as I sat quietly before the service began, when Victoria tapped me on the shoulder, I felt a sense of support. Her short dark hair and well-cut suit gave her an air of ease and authority. As petite as she is, no more than 5'2" in heels, her presence comes across large. Yet there are still remnants of the former first-grade teacher in the way she greets parishioners with a warm smile and quick sense of humor.

When I told her of the visit to the surgeon today, she squeezed my shoulder, and in her kind, gentle way said, "Let's talk after the service."

During our conversation, she gave me her home phone number and made me promise to call her as soon as I had seen the doctor.

Victoria's number is scribbled on a piece of paper on the car seat next to me. I really shouldn't bother her. It's her day off, and she doesn't want to hear about my troubles on her day off. She doesn't even know me. She did say to call, but then my mother always said, "Don't impose." God forbid I offend or bother somebody on a day off.

The gum-snapping clerk in the convenience store stares at me through the window. I can't just sit here paralyzed in the parking lot. My index finger punches in Victoria's number and hovers over the Send button. I either need to call her or go home and cry or go back to the office. Being out of options, I press Send.

"Victoria? This is Lynne. I'm really sorry to bother you on your day off. I just got out of the doctor's office, and it's not good news. He confirmed the cancer. I don't know what to do. I'm sitting in a convenience store parking lot and drinking a soda. Hal is in Taiwan. My parents are thousands of miles away. My friends are still at work, and I don't want to go to my office and pretend. You told me yesterday it was okay for me to call you."

She tells me to meet her at the church. "On your day off? I hate for you to come in on your day off, but I really would like to talk with someone." I told her I'd be there in ten minutes and offered up a prayer. "Thank you, God. First, I scream at you for letting this happen, and then I thank you for placing people like Victoria in my life."

At the church, I hope Victoria can't see my knees shaking as I walk into her office. She greets me with a smile and a hug that is surprisingly firm for someone so small. Even on her day off, her appearance is immaculate: tailored slacks, sweater, and silk scarf. "Let's start with a prayer," she says. The three-year-old in my head pipes up. "I don't want to start with a prayer. I want to start talking about me. I'm not even sure prayer will work at this point. Do you think God really cares?" Reluctantly, and because I really have no choice, I bow my head while Victoria prays. During the prayer, I begin to calm down and feel some of my hysteria start to dissipate. In a few minutes, I feel calm enough to speak rationally.

With a lump in my throat, knots in my stomach, and hands shaking, I tell her what the doctor said. I describe the feeling in my breast as my hand gently, almost unconsciously, rubs it over and over. As we speak, Victoria asks me to close my eyes and visualize my tumor. "Give it a shape. Give it a color. Give it a life of its own."

Slowly, I take a deep breath, close my eyes, and see an odd-shaped clump invading my body. It is red with blue tentacles. It looks like one of those brains with things sticking out all over it that they show in science fiction movies. I can see it snaking its way through my body. I name it "Harry" and tell him, "I don't like you. Get out of my body!" A shiver shimmies down my spine and tears run down my checks.

Victoria says, "Picture it shrinking, Lynne. Take away its power. Picture God reaching in and squeezing it down to nothingness."

"Victoria, this feels silly. It is seems like nothing but a lot of psychological mumbo jumbo."

But I do it anyway. The tumor draws in its tentacles like someone drawing in limbs. To my surprise, I begin to feel some of my mental strength returning. My visualizing is interrupted by Victoria's voice. "Lynne, you can influence the direction of this journey. I am not going to sit here and tell you that you are going to live. I am going to tell you that you might die. But it's your choice to decide how you're going to take this journey, how this is going to impact you and your family."

This makes absolutely no sense to me, but I don't argue. She continues, "My first husband died of cancer. I watched him go through the same anguish you're experiencing. Then, he arrived at a place where he was able to let go of the final result. He accepted his fate and turned the results of his journey over to God."

"But Victoria, I don't want peace with dying. I want life. I want this to go away. I want it to end tomorrow. I can't turn to God for peace. I'm not sure I even like God at this point. I'm angry. I'm scared. I want to live, not die with peace."

As Victoria listens to my fears, more tears roll down my cheeks. "How do I hide this from my children? This entire last weekend, my imagination ran wild. I couldn't stop crying. Sooner or later, they're going to see my tears and wonder what's going on. What am I going to tell them about the biopsy on Thursday? I can hide the tests because they're being done while the kids are in school, but it's going to be pretty hard to hide an operation."

"Lynne, go home and tell them tonight. Don't put it off another minute. Do you really think they don't know something's wrong? Do you think they don't see you crying and wonder what's happening to you?"

I suddenly have so many regrets about time spent traveling and working. Regrets about being in some European hotel instead of with my kids. Guilt over those two-in-the-morning phone calls from Keaton saying, "Mommy, can I tell you about school today?"

I regret the missed after-school trips to the zoo and fall walks in the park. I should have been sharing that with Dana and Keaton, not the nanny. I regret so much time spent on my career, always putting off that special time with my husband and children. I always believed there would be time for us to do things together in the future. Now there may not be a future.

I twist my wedding band around and around on my finger. Not a flaw in the circle of gold. No beginning or end. "Victoria, how can I tell them? What do I tell them? I don't know the outcome of this. I can't tell them I'm going to be okay when I don't know I'm going to be okay. I'm the mother. Aren't I supposed to have answers? Aren't mothers invincible? I can't tell them I'm scared or that I might die. What can I say?"

"How about the truth?" Victoria says. She makes it sound so simple. "How about telling them what you told me? You have a lump. It may be cancer. The doctors are going to do some tests this week. It means you will be in the hospital Thursday for a small operation. And you may be sick for a while."

Maybe I am making too much of this. Maybe it isn't as bad as it sounds.

On the way home, I decide to wait and speak with the children when Hal comes home. I can put away my tears and panic for forty-eight hours. I can do this. I am the mother.

Tuesday morning dawns. I go through the normal routine of getting the kids off to school and make a quick call to the office before heading to the hospital for a bone scan, blood tests, and a liver scan. I am terrified as I walk into the lab with wobbly knees. People look at me on the outside and think I am always in control. I give the appearance of not being affected by what is happening around me. What they don't realize is that deep down inside, my three-year-old is trembling and quaking.

Waiting to be called, I pretend to read a magazine while my mind races and fear invades my heart. Once in the lab, the wiry-haired technician looks at me and says, "We're going to inject this dye into your veins for the bone scan." He then injects a needle, and some sort of fluorescent dye flows into my veins. "This takes about two hours to work its way through your body," he says. "So you can go eat some lunch, read a book, and then come back for the scan."

The thought of lunch nauseates me. How in the world am I going to eat lunch? How am I going to read a book? Two hours? Two hours of sitting on my hands and waiting. Going to the office flashes through my mind. No, I'm not going to the office. I don't care how much work I have. Instead, I go to a nearby store and wander aimlessly, trying not to think about the scan, but the store is small and the aisles narrow, the clothing racks packed in tight. I have heard terrible things about putting people into those narrow scan tubes. I have never thought of myself as claustrophobic, but the power of suggestion is getting to me. It's all I can do to exit the store in a calm and orderly fashion and walk, not run, to my car even though my heart is primed for a sprint. A few minutes in the car and my shallow breath comes a little deeper and then steadies. Today, my goal is making it through the day with my sanity intact.

Back at the hospital, the wiry-haired technician leads me in for the bone scan. "Lie down on this table," he says with a broad smile meant to put me at ease.

"The skinny table that feeds into that long narrow tube?" I say. Ugh. Maybe with my eyes closed I can pretend I am lying on a bed.

"Once you're part way in the tube," he says, "you'll be able to see your bones glow on that TV monitor." He is all enthusiasm, like glowing bones are the coolest thing ever. I suppose they might be if they belonged to someone else.

As my body enters the confines of the tube, the memory of being sixteen and lying on a similar table in a screen cage for an electromylogram hits me with such force that I can barely breathe. I vividly remember the crackle and pop of the machine, the technician inserting needles carrying electrical charges into my muscles, hearing, as if it were now, the detachment of his voice as he ordered me over and over to "contract." With each effort, excruciating pain shot through whichever muscle was being tested. Tears streamed down my checks, but I would not cry out. Instead, I prayed for the agony to end. Over the course of those two years in the hospital, I repeated that same agonizing test every four months.

As my mind snaps back to the present, the bone scan technician tries to calm me down with friendly chatter.

"Are you trained in psychology?" I ask.

"No," he says, "not at all."

"Too bad. You should be."

Looking a little puzzled, he says, "We're going to start the test now. Just lie here, and go to sleep if you want. Or you can watch on the monitor."

The battery of tests takes most of the day, and when they are all completed, I head to the office. I go straight to my boss and break the news to him. Bless his heart. He is one of the kindest and gentlest men I know. Instead of going into a panic over the Bangkok meeting, he expresses only concern for me. I am the one who mentions that Bangkok is only three days away and I have to find a substitute. After some deliberation, Carl, our sales rep in San Francisco with the occasional international sales meeting thrown in, draws the short straw. He has no familiarity with this new product, but he's a technical wizard who can figure out enough from the specs to sell the pants off of it. A set of slides sent by courier and "Good luck" is all the preparation I give him. At this point, quite frankly, while I am eternally grateful to Carl for his willingness to step in at the last minute, I don't give a hoot about the exciting new product introduction or how the meeting is going to go. Carl is on his own.

On Wednesday, Hal arrives home, and for once I don't mind the pens and pencils in his pocket protector jabbing me as we hug. The reassurance of his bear-like arms wrapped around me and his calm in the face of crisis give me hope that anything is possible.

Hal calls Dana and Keaton into the family room. Sheba, true to the breed of Shepherd, herds them from behind, big ears straight up, eyes alert. Keaton heads for the television, but seeing Hal and me seated around the sofa, Sheba cuts him off and gently nudges him our direction. "She's right," Hal says. "Leave the TV and come sit down."

Keaton falls back into the sofa, while Dana plops on the far end, away from her brother. Sheba presents herself for a pat and then circles three times before she curls her light brown bulk on the floor between my feet and Hal's.

I'm thankful the kids are fourteen and eleven rather than seven and four. Theoretically, that should make this easier. I stammer at first, not sure what to say. So I start with, "I went to the doctor's for a checkup the other day, and they found a small bump in my breast." I can tell by their faces that a bump in the breast means nothing. "I've already had some tests," I continue. "And they're going to do more, but in the meantime, I have to go to the hospital tomorrow for a small operation to remove the bump."

My hands are clammy. I'm not doing this very well. The kids are staring. This woman who stammers and cries is not the mother they know. Even Sheba senses the difference. She pushes herself to sitting and then rests her head on my lap. The last bit of what I have to say tumbles out on an exhale. "The doctors will examine the bump under a microscope to see what it is. There's a chance it might be cancer."

Keaton pipes up. "Mom, I don't know what cancer is. Jason's mom died of cancer, and isn't that what grandma died of last year? Does this mean you might die? Is cancer worse than the flu?"

Inside, I am withering. Discussing something like this with our children is foreign to me. I have never discussed myself and my fears with my children. What a frightening experience. Up until now, I have assumed that a parent has to speak on a different level, has to hide fear, has to know which way the road will turn. Part of me wants to be the mother who is in complete control and able to reassure her children that this is absolutely nothing. Another part of me desperately needs my family gathering around me and showing me support and love and care. That Keaton wouldn't know what cancer is never occurred to me. I just assumed they both knew. But, then, why would they? Cancer is what Grandma had–Grandma who was seventy-five years old and lived so far across the country the kids hardly knew her. Jason's mom died before Keaton and Jason became friends, so there was no person to associate with the disease. Cancer is only a word to Keaton, a word that applies to old people or other people.

Meanwhile, Dana says nothing. The girl of a million questions sits on the couch and quietly listens. I would lay odds she has already made the connection between the outcome of her grandma's cancer and the prospect for mine.

"Keaton, cancer is a disease that makes your cells grow very fast. Many, many people get cancer, and most of them don't die. Grandma died because she wouldn't let the doctors take care of her. But I don't think that's going to happen to me. I'll only be in the hospital for a day, and then we'll have to wait a couple of more days to see what the tests show. The worst that will probably happen is that I'll need a second operation and some medicine."

Given his engineering background, Hal, with his yellow legal pad and ballpoint pen always at the ready, is very factual. Under stress, he loves to spout statistics. He jumps in with, "Women who find round, hard, cancerous lumps the size of a pea have a ninety-five-percent survival rate. Mommy is going to be just fine."

A noble statistic. Unfortunately, my cancer is the size of a golf ball and not round and hard but diffuse, and the doctors have hedged against giving any odds on my survival.

When Keaton's eyes glaze over, Hal spares us the numbers and plows on a little lighter. "Lots of people get cancer and take a few pills. Statistics show most cancer patients are cured."

I marvel that he is so matter of fact and not blithering like I am. "Look," I say, "I don't know the outcome of this journey, but, whatever it is, you're part of it. I'm your wise and wonderful mother, and I have no answers. I am afraid. I have no idea where this will take us. I can only say that we have started a journey, and I want you to take my hand and walk by my side. We may have different destinations, and, if you take this journey with me, we will go together as far as possible. If the time comes when the road must split and we must go in different directions, we will be ready, and we will look back and say the journey was a good one."

Tears hang on the rims of Dana's eyes, and Keaton won't even look at me. "I love you and need to know you're not worrying about me. Besides, you know me–I always bounce back quickly." I stop short of saying I'll be just fine. "Look at it this way. I don't have to go to Bangkok tomorrow. I get to stay home. Now that in itself is a benefit, right?"

Dana, being fourteen, has heard more about breast cancer than Keaton. Perching on the edge of the sofa, she wipes her eyes with the heel of her palm. Her deep brown eyes penetrate the fear behind my wobbly smile and attempt at lightheartedness. "Mom, how many women get breast cancer? Is this the same kind Grandma had? Do you think I can come to the hospital with you tomorrow? I can sit in your room with you. Please, can I skip school to be there?"

My eyes connect with Hal's. It's clear Dana's already made up her mind to be there, and though I'd like to spare her seeing me so vulnerable, the comfort of having her with me wins out. I give Hal a brief nod, and to Dana I say, "Of course."

We all turn to Keaton, who is sunk deep into the back of the sofa. "What about you, Keaton? Do you want to be there, too?" Hal asks.

Keaton sits on his hands, his eyes fixed on his lap. Without hesitation, he says, "No, hospitals scare me."

Chapter Five

How much time and human sharing are
lost because of the when and then?

That night, I climb into bed and shout at God. "Okay, God, Sunday school and church have been a big part of my life. I've done all the 'right' things, so now it's payback time. I dare you not to take care of me. You owe me. Furthermore, I have no intention of leaving this planet. End of discussion. Amen."

Years ago, I heard a joke about a little girl who took a test in school and answered a question by stating that Boston was the capitol of Vermont. That night as she finished her prayers, she begged, "God, please make Boston the capitol of Vermont." I am asking him to do the same for me, demanding he do whatever is necessary to make this come out the way I want.

I want sleep but manage to witness each hour slip by until the alarm finally goes off on Thursday morning. Biopsy day. I had hoped to get the biopsy over with early, but the only time available was in the afternoon. I don't even have to be at the hospital until 1:00. By 8:30, I've made breakfast, fed Sheba, cleaned up the kitchen, driven the kids to school—all in good cheer, as normal as can be, except for my reminder to Keaton to go to his day care after school because the rest of us will be at the hospital. Hal and I knock around the house for a bit in silence. He's restless, and I would just as soon have some time for myself. So I send him off to do the million things hanging over his head at the office. "Be back to pick you up at noon," he says on his way out the door.

I try focusing on reading, television–anything–as the time drags by. My only solace is Sheba, who paces the floor with me. It feels good to be alone and not have to worry about anyone watching, or commenting on, my restless behavior.

At the hospital, I try to act very casual, as if I'm not stepping through an unlit threshold, destination unknown. Two of my friends show up and give me a big white fluffy teddy bear. How long has it been since I hugged a teddy bear? International executives don't usually carry one around, but boy does this feel good. I want my Mommy. I want out of this bed. I want out of this situation.

Soon, I am pried loose from my family and friends, my wedding ring, even my teddy bear. I feel completely stripped of self. White ceiling tiles whip by in a blur overhead as the orderly wheels my bed down the hall. His stomach growls, but he doesn't acknowledge it or me for that matter. I'm forced to turn to the only thing I have left. "Okay, God, last chance to redeem yourself here. You give me life, and I'll give you the best I've got." The last thing I hear is not God's answer but the anesthesiologist telling me to count down from ten to one.

When I come out of the anesthesia, Hal, Dana, and my friends are standing in the room. They hand me my teddy bear and wait patiently while I drift in and out of sleep for another hour. Once I'm awake for more than fifteen minutes, the nurse takes my vitals, gives me a tiny cupful of soda and her blessing for a speedy recovery.

During the car ride home, I am nauseated and head straight for my bed as soon as I walk through the door. We have no answers about the cancer at this point and won't for another week. I sleep hard, but part of me hangs on the edge of consciousness and waits for the phone to ring and the doctor to confirm that his diagnosis is all a big mistake.

During the next week, our family tries to live a normal life and somehow keeps speculation at bay while we wait. My new motto becomes "Let's not jump to conclusions." Because we have no concrete information, I stick to hoping for the best and assume that everything will be fine. This works for maybe five minutes. Unlike the movies where everyone hugs and comes together with reassuring words of support and encouragement, we begin fighting over nonsense things. Dana, pick up your room. Lynne, stop yelling at the kids. Keaton, stop talking back to your father. Hal, stop with the statistics. We shout at each other constantly while fear runs rampant in our house. No one is able to comfort anyone. Hal and I try to reassure the kids when we are not feeling the least bit reassured ourselves.

One night before going to sleep, I turn to Hal. "What if I don't make it? What if I die?" For nearly twenty years of married life, Hal has been very predictable in dealing with crises. He loves statistics and charts. I hate them. "I really don't think you're going to die. I've read the statistics on breast cancer, and you have a very good chance of survival," he says. On goes the light, and out comes a yellow legal pad. As soon as I see this yellow paper, I cringe and know that I am in for a long, boring lecture about percentages.

"Lynne, look." He taps his ballpoint on the pad and rapidly sketches out a graph. "I read that these are the number of women who have had lumps x size, and this is how many lived. Here are the women who had larger lumps, and this is how long they lived." On and on he goes with the statistics.

I know he is trying to reassure me, but I get irritated, "Hal, I don't care about those numbers. I don't want to look at the yellow paper. Can't I just tell you I'm scared without getting an encyclopedia full of facts and figures thrown in my face? Look what happened to your mother. She died. Where did she fit on your little chart? I have cancer. People die from cancer. Not everyone lives. Admit it. You're afraid I'll die, too. Instead of numbers, let's talk about the kids and you. I want to make sure the kids are okay. I don't want you to remarry and have the kids wind up with some twenty-year-old blonde bombshell as their mother."

One glance up from the yellow pad, along with a chuckle at the reference to the type of woman I think he might select, and he changes his tactic. "Okay, okay. I won't remarry some sexy, young thing. But Lynne, you are not going to die. My mother died because she didn't go to a doctor until it was well advanced—far more advanced than yours—

and my mother didn't take any treatments. Mark my word for it; you're going to live."

I turn to him and say, "I sure hope you're right, Hal. Having your mother die last year has really scared the kids, and it's scared me." He finally puts down the yellow pad and turns out the light. He says, "I just wish she'd done something to take care of herself. I wish she had let them operate on her. But she watched her own mother die of cancer and always believed it was the treatments that made it worse. She was determined not to have any treatments whatsoever. Believe me, Lynne; that's not going to happen to you. You're getting the operation. You're getting treatment. You're going to be okay. You'll see."

The next several days plod. We pace. We fret. We argue. We go to the movies–anything to pass the time until we learn how extensive the cancer is and what will happen next. I hope Hal is right. I am on a bullet train I didn't ask to get on, and I see no way off. I'm scared. Scared of the future, scared of the chemotherapy, scared I won't live to celebrate another birthday. Doctor Holmes's edict, "We're not doing these tests to determine whether you have cancer," rings in my ears. Yet I sit here hoping he is wrong, that he's going to tell me it's all a mistake. I anticipate his call, his chagrin as he says, "You know how I was so positive this was cancer? Well, ha ha, looks like I made one of the few mistakes of my career. Sorry about that."

I am a strong believer in traditional medicine. I actually know nothing of alternative or holistic medicine, other than a few things I have picked up here and there. It is pretty hard to live in a place like Oregon and not hear about it. But to me, alternative medicine is something that those people use–certainly not senior managers like me. In my mind, those people are a little nuts.

One by one, strangers I encounter tell me about using meditation, massage, and a low-fat diet as part of the healing process. "Eat more foods with antioxidants," I am told. What in the world are antioxidants? "Meditate daily," someone tells me. Me? Meditate? You have to be joking. Walking through the bookstore, I find a book on meditation and glance around to see if anyone is watching before I lift it off the shelf. Do top executives meditate and read this stuff? I wonder whether it really works.

The night I buy the meditation book, I climb in bed and open it to the first page. After reading a few pages, I close my eyes and try some of the meditations. I'm worried that my kids or husband will come into the room and think I am weird, so I turn out the light so they won't see me. During the first exercise, I fall into a peaceful sleep. Drifting off, a voice in my head says, "If someone tells me that baying at the moon every night will get me well, I'll do it."

When I was pregnant, the whole world looked pregnant. Now is no different. Have there always been this many books and tapes and movies about cancer? I had better get busy reading and listening. I will leave no stone unturned. If it worked for even one person, I'll try it.

Reading book after book about survivors, one thing becomes evident. Almost without fail, those cancer victims who survive terrible odds take charge of their lives spiritually and holistically. Traditional medicine takes care of them physically, but at the same time, they make major spiritual changes, trust a higher power, and begin taking very good care of their bodies. When was the last time I walked a mile other than running for an airplane? When was the last time I took time for myself and told others "no"? When was the last time I actually sat down at a table and ate lunch instead of eating off the dashboard of the car? I don't know the answer to any of these questions.

The phone interrupts my daydreaming. Victoria asks whether I have heard anything. "No, I have an appointment at 11:00 to find out where we go next. I keep hoping they'll say they made a mistake."

"Is Hal going with you to the doctor's?"

"No, he wanted to come, but he had a pretty important meeting, and I suggested he go to work. I reassured him I would call him as soon as I talked with Dr. Holmes. I prefer hearing what the doctor has to say on my own, and then I'll report back to everyone else. I guess I just keep trying to act as if this is no big deal."

At five minutes to 11:00, I arrive at the surgeon's office. Once again, I am early. I haven't arrived early for anything in years, and now I am showing up at every doctor's appointment and test five or ten minutes early. I pretend to read but with the concentration of a three-year-old holding the book upside down in her lap. After a short wait, I hear, "Okay, Lynne. It's your turn."

Doctor Holmes walks in and peers at me over his half-glasses. He takes a deep breath while I hold mine. "We didn't find any clean tissue, Lynne. Normally, we take out the tumor and some surrounding tissue and hope we get all the cancer, but this went all the way to the margins. The type of cancer you have is called infiltrating lobular carcinoma. It doesn't form a distinct lump. Instead, it has a small core that sends tentacles throughout the breast. We don't know yet whether it has spread. This kind of cancer is usually very invasive. You are going to have to have your entire breast removed. Because this type of cancer normally shows up in both sides, we recommend having both breasts removed as well as the lymph nodes."

I sit in a stupor and say nothing. I am afraid of losing all control. My mind is completely numb, and part of me simply doesn't believe what I am hearing. What can I say? "Give me an aspirin, and send me home"? I decide it is better to say nothing than to open my mouth and become hysterical. I try to act very professional and stay focused on medical phrases such as "very high S phase," "not estrogen positive," and "aggressive"—all indicators that lead to a poor prognosis.

"If you want any chance of survival, Lynne, your left breast has to go. As for the right, at this point, we don't see any sign of cancer, but because lobular carcinoma is so invasive, it's almost certain it will show up there. I'd like to schedule the surgery for next week. Meanwhile, I'll recommend an oncologist who will start you on a chemotherapy program following the surgery. You should talk to her right away."

This isn't what is supposed to happen. This can't be happening to me. I want reassurances. I want to hear my doctor say, "We think this is really nothing, but we want to be cautious." All my hopes are being slaughtered.

"Look," I say, "you doctors are going to control my life for the rest of my life. I need some time to sort this out. My daughter's eighth-grade graduation is in three weeks. I want to be well for that. So I'd like to wait three weeks—three weeks to sort out what is happening to me, three weeks to get through her graduation. And I want three weeks to check you out, to decide whether you and the other doctors know what you're talking about. If this cancer has been in my body for two years, three more weeks won't matter."

Dr. Holmes peers over the top of those half-glasses with his kind smile. "Okay. We can wait that long. Let's schedule the surgery three weeks from today—but not a minute longer. That's as long as I dare let this go."

As soon as I get home, I dial up Dr. Schrinsky, the gynecologist who referred me to Dr. Holmes, the surgeon. Naturally, he is busy, and I leave a message and ask him to call me as soon as possible. It seems like an eternity before he calls me back. "Dan, have you heard what's happening? Have you talked with Dr. Holmes? Have you heard about the results of my tests? Dan, who is this guy? Why'd you refer me to him? Did he give you his card at a cocktail party and say, 'By the way, if you ever have a patient with breast cancer, send her my way. I'd like to do a mastectomy now and then'? What are his qualifications? Can he save my life?"

Dr. Schrinsky chuckles and, in a voice I have known for fifteen years, reassures me and says, "Lynne, he's one of the top three surgeons in Portland. When I recommended him, I did a little bit of a personality match. I think you two are a good fit. Believe me; you're in excellent hands."

Talking to Dan has made me feel much better, and I feel reassured knowing I have some very good doctors who care about me. But I am still very skeptical, so I call my family physician, Dr. Lea. Two days later, I am sitting across from him and am learning that he, too, has had cancer—testicular cancer. He has been undergoing radiation and seems more than willing to share stories with me. I feel as if I am talking with the old country doctor who has nothing but time for me. I ask him, "Do you know Dr. Holmes? Is he any good? Should I trust him?"

Dr. Lea patiently waits for me to finish my barrage of questions and then quietly responds, "You could not be in better hands. He is one of the finest surgeons in the Portland area. You can relax and trust him."

One phenomenon about cancer is being thrown into a circle of doctors and specialists you do not know. Over the years, I got to know my regular doctors. I built up a trust in them, but something major like cancer thrusts you into a group of complete strangers. You say, "How do you do?" and immediately follow it with "Can you save my life?"

After I leave Dr. Lea's office, I know I have to call my parents and two sisters. My parents react as predicted. The audible gasp. The talk about booking the next plane from Atlanta. "Please, don't come just yet. Wait until the surgery. Then you can help us. Hal, Dana, Keaton, and I need time right now as a family. I know you mean well, but this is a time for us to be together."

The disappointment in the silence on the other end is palpable. "I do have a big favor," I say.

"Anything," my parents respond in unison.

"Mother, you know a slew of doctors, and Daddy, you've played golf with most of them. If you really want to do something, talk to them and find out what they say about this type of cancer. See whether you can dig up any new information."

My mother immediately reminds me that Danny Clarke, the kid I used to baby-sit for when he was six years old, is now a radiologist working in a large cancer center in Virginia. "What's his phone number? I'll call him tomorrow."

Danny, who is now called Dan, asks me a thousand technical questions I can't answer. Instead, I give him the phone number of Dr. Holmes and Dr. Fielder, the oncologist. "Lynne, I'll call them tomorrow and discuss this with them. In the meantime, it's really important that you take care of your body. I believe we all have cancer cells in our bodies, and our immune system destroys them. If the immune system is weak, though, the cancer cells are allowed to grow out of control. Make sure you get a lot of rest, eat well, and do everything you can to boost your body's defenses. Don't drink any alcohol." There's a pause before he says, "By the way, do you ever meditate?" Meditate? Me? This from an M.D.? Maybe the holistic people aren't so dumb after all.

While I wait for Dan to make his calls, I gather every book on cancer survival I can find. One of these books is written by a local woman who was given less than a one percent chance of surviving liver cancer. She told her doctors she did not want to hear anything about percentages or statistics. All she wanted to know was whether it was possible to survive. If just one person survived, then she knew there was hope for her. Sounds good to me. If she made it, so can I. No more statistics. No more long faces. Just believing in survival.

Out of nowhere, I am introduced to a woman who is a cancer patient fighting her second bout with breast cancer. She personally knows the liver cancer patient who wrote the book and gives me the name of her doctor. He is at the medical school here in Portland. "Okay, I'm calling him tomorrow," I declare.

As soon as I ask for an appointment, I am told he is not taking any new patients, but I refuse to be turned away. "I want only one hour of his time. I don't want to become a patient of his. I want to talk to him and see whether he agrees with my diagnosis and proposed treatment. Surely, he has one hour in the next three weeks." A miracle occurs. The receptionist says, "I can get you in a week from Tuesday. Bring all your test results and x-rays." I got the appointment! Yea, God.

My family is annoyed I am doing this. For the most part, I trust the doctors I have seen up to this point. But this is my life at stake. I am a smart businesswoman and a scientist, yet a part of me is still in denial. Deep down, I keep hoping one of the doctors will disagree with the diagnosis.

Two weeks have now passed, and all of the doctors agree. It is only one more week before the proposed double mastectomy, and Hal is having difficulty with the prospect of removing my right breast as well as the left. Because it has no sign of cancer, it seems wrong somehow to whack it off. Hal decides he wants to discuss the decision with the surgeon.

This turns into a bit of an argument. "How can you second-guess Dr. Holmes?" I ask. "He's supposed to be one of the best, and if he says both breasts have to be removed, I believe him. Why don't you? I don't want a double mastectomy either if it isn't necessary, but I don't want to disagree with the doctors at this point." Hal makes a move for the yellow pad. A ballpoint pen slides out of his pocket protector. The pen's simple click sends me into a frenzy. "I'm going to call Dr. Holmes and discuss it with him," he says.

Arguing with an engineer is futile. Hal, calm to the core, finds Dr. Holmes's phone number and calls, not caring that it's 2:00 on a Saturday afternoon. After they have spoken for almost an hour, Hal calls from the other room, "Lynne, get on the phone. Dr. Holmes and I want to talk to you."

"Oh, Dr. Holmes, I'm so sorry Hal's bothering you about this, but he's adamant that the double mastectomy may not be necessary."

We continue talking to him for another hour and try to sort it all out and dissect all of the technical information. Hal has been doing his homework, and the two of them are speaking as peers.

"We know you said this diagnosis is for both breasts, but it doesn't make much sense to take off the right breast if it shows only good tissue," Hal says. I take advantage of their brief silence to push on. "Instead of removing it, can you just do a biopsy and then make the decision? If it shows anything suspicious, then of course I'll agree to have it removed."

After much debate, Dr. Holmes says, "Lynne, you and Hal seem to be well aware of the risks. You know the chances are very high that the cancer's going to occur in the right breast and that the standard treatment is to remove them both. I know you're promising to get your check-ups regularly, but patients often promise, and then as time goes by, they start missing appointments. Rather than risk someone not following up, I've found it safer with this type of cancer to remove the nonmalignant breast at the same time as the malignant one."

"Can we agree on this? Because you're aware of the risk and are willing to be conscientious about check-ups for the next five years, I'll agree to do the biopsy on the right side at the time of the left mastectomy," Dr. Holmes continues. "If the biopsy shows anything positive, we can remove the right breast as soon as you've healed from the first surgery. If the tissue shows no actual malignancy, we'll watch it closely over a five-year period. Before you agree to this, however, you need to know that if the cancer appears in your right breast, we probably won't catch it early."

"Will you catch it in time?"

A sigh comes over the line. "I think so."

As we hang up the phone, Hal and I look at each other. We have more than enough facts to take a calculated risk, and emotionally, all I can cope with right now is the loss of one breast. Is this the right decision? In the long run, perhaps yes and perhaps no. However, I believe that we understand the risk we are taking and are making a conscious decision to take this route. I know that I can have the breast removed in a month if the biopsy is positive, and I know that I can have it removed in the future if anything even remotely suspicious shows up in my check-ups.

The few days before surgery, I am still shaking my fist at God and making demands. Yet, when I feel totally lost, an answer to a question or an insight appears from nowhere. Amazing coincidences occur, and I begin to see strange phenomena taking place. I accidentally bump into a person who can give me precisely the answer I need at the time I need it. Events are crashing together at exactly the right time. Could God actually be acting as a tour guide on this journey?

As I surrender control, my family and I continue this journey through the unknown, a journey that is proving to be full of life, full of laughter, full of sharing, and full of spontaneous moments. It is also filled with fear, anger, and lots of crying.

It's funny what cancer does to people. It makes the then and when so very important in the now. All that matters is how we live each day. We can no longer wait for the when, and we have to forget about the then. We must move together into the now: a now that is frightening, a now that I don't want to be part of.

Life is changing now, before my very eyes, into a when that is uncertain, a when that says more pain is on the way. This when says, "I want the then, a then of children laughing and growing, a then that held a glorious future, a then that said 'Shoot for the stars.'"

Now just give me life. Never mind the stars. Just give me today and tomorrow. Give them to me without pain, without sadness, and without fear. Make my now be all that I want. Fill my now with joy, with those I care about. Let me take the time to show them now that I care. There may not be a when.

How much time and human sharing are lost because of the when and then? Give me another chance now to share, care, and live.

Chapter Six

*I start saying "no" to those who will see
my death as an inconvenience and
"yes" to those who will mourn me.*

The surgery is getting closer, and it's time to tell my friends. What do I say to all the people I have been too busy to speak with, too busy to write to? Embarrassment overwhelms me. I have been so busy with my "important" work and my "important" travel that I haven't spoken with most of my friends in months, maybe even a year, and for some, probably several years. What am I going to say? I realize now how big a part of my life they have been, and I simply lost contact with them. Now, they are more important than ever.

I feel awkward calling them out of the blue when my purpose in calling isn't to ask how they are and how their families are but instead to tell them I am scared, that I am not okay, that I need them.

I suddenly realize that I have lived mostly for myself: too busy, too many trips, too many "me" things. Yet others found time for me. They found time to write, call, say hello. Now I want them back in my life. I want to recapture that which brought us together in the first place. I want them to know that even though I haven't been in touch, I have thought of them and have enjoyed their cards and letters and phone calls. I always cared, but they didn't know, did they? Will they care that I cared, or is it too late?

There were times I heard about a friend's suffering or pain, and all I could manage was, "I'm sorry. I have a plane to catch. Hope it gets better." Ashamed of my carelessness, I now feel the pain of others and care when they hurt. I realize it is my friends who will mourn me. It is my family and friends who will suffer, and yet I have been too busy to spend time with them. I assumed I would always have time in the future.

God, give me another chance to show my friends how much they mean to me. I want this journey to be full of laughter, sharing, and spontaneous moments. I know it is also going to be filled with fear, anger, and lots of crying. But, God, help me to put cancer in the back seat. Soon, the surgery will be over, and all that matters is how we as family and friends are going to live each day. Please help us not to wait for the when. Help us to forget about then. Help us to learn to live in the now.

The phone calls begin. Of course, my friends assume I am calling just to say hello, and initially I am too embarrassed to tell them otherwise. They chitchat about their lives. Then, after catching up on all their news, they ask, "What's happening with you?"

The word "cancer" falls with the same effect as a bomb. Boom! Silence and then some stuttering and then usually "Wow. What are the doctors saying?" Occasionally, my friends try to deny the situation. "Oh, they must be mistaken. I'm sure you're just fine. My aunt (or cousin or coworker) had cancer, and she's just great." I want to scream, "Well, I'm not! Cancer isn't generic! Just because your aunt or cousin Joe or whoever didn't die doesn't mean I won't!" Because I'm convinced I am going to die, I assume everyone else should be just as convinced. When my friends say something optimistic, instead of being grateful, I get irritated that they aren't taking my impending death seriously enough.

Amazingly, my true friends hang in there in spite of my irrational thinking. A major shift begins to occur. I start saying "no" to those who will see my death as an inconvenience and "yes" to those who will mourn me. My friends rally: cooking, cleaning, and nurturing. They say, "We're so glad you're back in our lives, so glad we have a chance to help you."

I've never let friends be close to me. I've had people who said they were friends, and I've had people who acted like friends. But what really is a friend? To me it's always been someone I said "hi" to in the store. Someone with whom I played cards, for whom I fixed dinner. Someone I got together with for a movie. But someone inside my heart? Not me. I don't let people inside my heart. Being stuck in that hospital for so long as a teenager caused me to form a shell I don't let people penetrate. Now, friends are all around saying, "We care. We care whether you live or die. We care. We care. "

How lucky can I be? In business, I spend time with people who will probably step over me when I am dead and say, "Oh, what a shame. Now let's get that new project going. Meeting at 2:00." People at work like me because I am good at what I do. But why do my friends, who don't know me professionally, care whether I live or die? How could I have ever thought a job or a career or a trip to Bangkok could be better than this? I am happier when I am embraced by the arms and love of my family and friends than I am with any career choices or outstanding performance review. Why have I wasted all this time trying to be someone important to the world when I have so many important people at home who love me and to whom I am already important? It is my friends who will mourn me, my family and friends who will suffer. My assumption has been that I would have time for them when life in the fast lane settled down.

What do I offer my friends that I am unable to offer myself? Why does it matter to them whether I live or die, that I am hurting? Is it a social thing? An obligation? Or is there some one thing I give them that they would miss? Something I alone offer that fills a void in their hearts?

Last year in a European train station, I saw a woman crying. My heart ached when I saw her; her tears felt so sad. I took the chance she would understand English and offered her a tissue. She smiled sadly when I asked whether I could help, and told me she had been robbed. She had lost all her money in what, for her, was a foreign country. I got into a taxi with her and took her to the Croatian Embassy where someone would take care of her. Before I left, she asked why I bothered to help her. "I am a stranger in a foreign land," she said.

"No," I said. "We're not strangers. We're friends who simply haven't met."

Is that a friend? Someone who hurts when you have tears in your eyes? Someone whose stomach aches when sharing your laughter? Someone who knows you better in the first minute you meet than you might know yourself in a lifetime? Discovering true friendship feels wonderful. It feels strange. It is joyful and scary at the same time. My friends say, "Take my hand. You don't have to walk this path alone anymore. You don't have to earn it. You don't have to measure it. Just take the hand that's reaching out in care."

Will they see me the same way when a part of me is gone and my body is a different shape? When my hair is gone, will I still be loved? I want my friends to help me see what it is they see in me. I'm blind right now. I need them to open my eyes.

My minister, Victoria, told me the first day we talked, "Some of the people you call friends and expect to be with you throughout this journey will indeed be with you. Some of them will disappear. On the other hand, people you least expect will come out of the woodwork and stay by your side." I was positive she was wrong, but she was right.

The head of my daughter's orchestra suddenly appeared at my house one day with food in hand and lots of friendly conversation. I had known her only at a distance. Conversely, a good friend with whom I have had dinner once a month for the past three years called exactly once when I was first diagnosed. Since then, our only communication has been messages passed on through mutual acquaintances. "Tell Lynne I'm sorry I haven't had time to call. Tell her I am thinking of her."

Asking people for help or favors is foreign to me. I always feel I'm imposing. Cancer hasn't made me feel any differently in this regard. Even though everyday someone says to me, "Let me know how I can help," chances are I am not going to call any of them.

Then, Mary called. "I know how independent you are," she said, "so here's what I'm going to do. Every time people say they want to help, write down their names and phone numbers. You won't call them, but I will. After the surgery, you give me the schedule of your chemotherapy treatments, and if Hal can't take you, I'll make certain someone takes you to the hospital and picks you up again. I'll have people cook meals for you and your family. Someone will do your laundry. Someone will shop for you. Just give me the names of every single person who wants to help."

My husband is greatly relieved because, while he wants to help, the thought of handling the kids, laundry, cooking, transportation, and taxi service for seven or eight months is a bit overwhelming. I am astounded that people we know well and people we hardly know at all are appearing on our doorstep. So many people care. It is rewarding yet difficult at the same time to have so many people around on a regular basis.

I am a loner, not used to constant companions sharing my thoughts and fears. For so many years, I have held people at a distance and have believed that my only value was the part of me that was smart and capable. I spent a lot of time worrying about what people thought of me and whether they liked me, always assuming they didn't. A friend once said, "How can people not like you? They don't even know you." For years, I dreamed of a day when my fears of not being liked would go away. I used to think that if I lived long enough, they would somehow magically disappear. Surely, people at eighty aren't worried about being liked. They wear purple. They spit in the street. Now I realize I may not live to eighty or sixty or even fifty-one. When am I going to let go of my fears? If I am going to die in a year, I want to experience what I have always fantasized a friendship to be. Talking together, sharing inner thoughts, laughing together. I have to do it now–before it is too late. I have to take the risk, or I may never experience this missing part of my life.

I still remember my first date with my husband. I was sitting in my most professional pose when he looked at me and, out of the blue, said, "You are really insecure. You put on this big front, and it turns out it's all a big facade."

I was shocked. "What are you talking about? This is who I am." I decided I intensely disliked him. Yet, for some reason, I continued to go out with him. On each date, he would probe and push into my soul.

Gradually, I began to feel safe sharing my feelings with him. But that safety never translated to other people–until now.

Suddenly, friendship takes on a new meaning. I want with others what I found with my husband many years ago. I no longer just want to fix dinner and chat. I no longer just want to go to the movies as friends. I want to walk down to the river together, share my dreams and hopes and what is in my heart. I want to run and cry and laugh in the sunshine and in the rain. Scream on roller coasters together. Share my tears and my fears and my joys and myself. I want to share the part of my heart that will soothe their hurts. I want to know and be known as a friend.

Chapter Seven

Does the Breast Have a Soul?

The thought of losing a part of my body will not penetrate my psyche. Whether it is a breast, a leg, or an arm, it is part of me, and I am part of it. Standing in front of the mirror these last days before the surgery, I stare at both breasts and try to picture what it will be like to have only one. I cover up the left breast and turn this way and that as if trying on a new dress. I force my eyes to look at the reflection of my breast. I want to look straight ahead into my own eyes, but my glance catches a glimpse of the breast that will soon take its leave. I find myself saying, "I'm sorry."

My parents have arrived and are fluttering all around me. I love them dearly, yet my mother has a hard time seeing me as an adult and tends to smother me. Often times I think she thinks I can't find my way out of a telephone booth.

One evening as my parents and I sit in the family room while dinner simmers on the stove, my mother leans forward on the couch and begins, "I knew I should have said something to you about all your traveling. This is all my fault. If only I'd said something to you, maybe you would have slowed down and gotten more rest. Then none of this would have happened. I'm sure all that traveling is what caused this."

Overstuffed couch cushions swallow my father's thin frame. He crosses an ankle over his knee, shakes opens the sports section, and sighs. Sheba pads in, circles three times, and then curls in close to my feet. The predictability of her warmth is a comfort.

"Mother, I really don't think there's a correlation. I'm fifty years old and take responsibility for my own life. None of this is your fault."

"Well, I can't tell you how awful I feel about this," Mother says. Her manicured hands clasp and unclasp, a gesture that has always irritated me. "How terrible it is that you're the one who's sick. You have two children, a family. It isn't fair. I've lived my life, raised my family. It should be me, not you. I'd give anything to have gotten the cancer instead. What's this family going to do without you? Hal can't raise the kids himself. He travels all the time, doesn't know how to cook. Oh, this is such a tragedy. If only it were me."

"For God's sake, Mother, I am not going to die." At the irritation in my voice, Sheba rises and begins to pace the space between my parents on the couch and me in my armchair. A sentry in the line of fire.

"This isn't a movie. I'm not going to drop dead any minute. I plan on living, Mother. I'm going to see my children graduated and married and, God willing, with children of their own. Besides, if, by chance, I don't live, Hal's very capable. He takes care of the kids when I'm on a trip. He'll take good care of them. Anyway, I'm not ready to talk about this. There's plenty of time to deal with the 'what ifs' when we have to."

The newspaper crumples to my father's lap, and he jumps in. "Well, Lynne, that's all fine and good, but you have to make plans. We need to talk about the kids, the house. We have a problem we have to discuss."

As my parents start giving their opinions about what we should do if I die, Hal, who has overheard the conversation, enters the room. At the sight of him, Sheba resumes her post at my side and sits, resting her head on my lap. Snookers is lying at my feet. Hal settles into his chair close to mine, calmly crosses his ankle over his knee, and says, "Lynne is not going to die."

My father checks his watch as if not only to dispute the statement but also to check and see the scheduled time remaining. Mother's hand wringing goes into overdrive. Out comes Hal's yellow pad. "Here, look at the statistics. The majority of women with breast cancer don't die"

My parents will not let this go, and soon the conversation escalates into a full-blown shouting match. My father turns to Hal and shouts, "Look, Hal, we have a problem here."

Hal, who is normally pretty calm, yells back, "No, we don't have a problem. Lynne and I have a problem. It's our problem, and we'll solve it like we solve all of our problems—on our own. Besides, Lynne isn't going to die." My mother's voice scales up several octaves. The martyr voice. The hair on the back of my neck comes to full attention at this tone of voice. Sheba pushes into my leg and rubs her ear against it, away from the sound. Mother's line about wishing it could be her instead of me is one I've heard all my life. Something as simple as me catching a cold because I didn't take a sweater with me when I went out became her fault because she didn't tell me to take it.

Bristling, I shout, "Well, you can't take this away. It is happening to me, and it's my disease." When I quiet down, I realize she is trying to show concern, and I feel guilty about snapping at her and my father. It has just been such a tense time for all of us, and on the surface, we are all acting as if nothing is wrong and are going about our daily chores.

This cancer has not come at a convenient time—not that anything of this nature ever does. My mind flashes back to my desk piled high with new brochures, manuals, and travel schedules. I am amazed at how fast the Bangkok meeting, the urgent crises in the office, and the demands of the outside world all disappear. What matters most is my survival. I have dropped everything, and for the first time I can remember, I have been saying "no" to tasks people expect of me and "no" to people with whom I simply do not want to spend time.

Instead, I spend my time focusing on what is important to me. For the first time in my career, I do not tell my family I have too much work to do or that I can't cook dinner for them or take the kids to a movie or spend an evening out with Hal. For the first time I say, "Work will wait; my family won't."

The day of the surgery, a rainy day in early June, arrives. As with the biopsy, I don't have to be at the hospital until noon, so we are all puttering around and acting as if we have something to keep us occupied. Shortly after getting up, I send Hal off to his office with his promise to meet me at the hospital at noon. I escape my fidgety parents and leave them to watch over a sleeping Dana and Keaton while I meet my close friend Lee for breakfast. Lee has known his share of hardship. A few years back, his sixteen-year-old son died of AIDS. I remember the months Lee spent with his son in hospice, his son's death, and the hole in Lee's life once the boy was gone.

Now Lee seems healed. He shovels in bacon and eggs at an alarming rate while my stomach roils in pre-surgery abstinence from food or drink of any kind. Like a broken record, I keep saying, "I don't want to do this. I want to be someplace else. I don't want to lose my breast. It's been with me all my life, and suddenly, it will be gone. Tonight, a part of me will be gone."

It's like knowing that within a few short hours I'll be in a plane crash. It is spooky to know that I will undergo such an incredible transformation in a few hours. Tears run down my checks. I am no longer putting on a face that says to the world, "I accept this." I do not. I am fighting for control every second that I sit here.

As I cry with my teary face buried on my folded arms, Lee reaches over and strokes my hair over and over, like a parent comforting a small child. "It's only skin," he says. "It's not important." But the tears continue. Having been in and around hospitals most of my life, I am not afraid of the surgery. My fear is losing a part of myself. "How do you know it is only skin, Lee? That I'll be the same person when this is over? What if I lose a part of who I am? Will I be a different person? Like a light switch going on and off?"

Lee doesn't know what to say to comfort me, so he starts cracking jokes. I am not sure he can say anything that will make me feel better. Hal finally has given up on trying to reassure me using the only way he seems to know, his statistics. I can't stand being treated like a statistic, and Lee's jokes feel like he is not taking this very seriously.

My anger and discontent with this whole situation have dissipated and have been replaced by a sadness unlike any I have ever felt. Because I am flying over open ocean, no land in sight, I can do nothing but tighten my seatbelt and pray.

Finally, it is time. We go home, and Lee trades places with my parents and the kids. Keaton has reluctantly agreed to come along but says he will not come into my room. Before we leave, the kids hand me a pillow in a bright green and purple dinosaur case. "Here, Mom. We thought you might like this at the hospital. It will remind you of home, and maybe it will make it not hurt so bad."

After meeting up with Hal and checking in at the front desk, I am taken to room 254, a number that will be forever burned in my memory. Everyone follows. Do all patients checking into the hospital have an entourage with them?

The first thing I do is put the kids' purple and green pillow on the bed, and then I peek into the bathroom and try to get a feel for these significant surroundings. Waiting for what comes next, my family tries to be cheerful, chattering idly. Not me. I am very restless. I feel something boiling up inside me that I can't quite put my finger on. "It's only skin" keeps reverberating in my brain. My mind is a long way from what is happening in this room.

Abruptly, I focus in, aware of a nurse trying to force a tranquilizer on me. "No, I don't want to take a tranquilizer," I say. "I'm not nervous. I don't think I need it."

She squints at me in a way that says, "Oh, boy, she's going to be one of those patients."

My mother pipes up. "Now, Lynne. Don't you think you should take the pill?"

"No. I don't want it. I want some time alone. How about you all going to get lunch? Have a soda, and let me have some time to myself."

In the silence that follows, it suddenly occurs to me. I know what I must do. I must say good-bye to my breast. I must acknowledge that it has been a part of me, and I am part of it.

Does the breast have a soul? Am I killing off something that is as much a living thing as I am? Is my soul in my breast? Is it in every cell of my body? Am I going to lose a part of my soul when I lose my breast? My mind starts to whirl, and I feel a surge of emotion that I want to write down. It is as if my soul is vomiting.

I search the hospital room, find an old envelope, and ask the nurse for a pencil. Again, she tries to get a tranquilizer down me. "You really should take this pill," she says. "This is major surgery, and it will calm you down."

"No, right now I don't need to calm down. I need to write down what is regurgitating from within."

It isn't just Lee who has told me my breast is only skin. Almost everyone has told me at some point, "It's only skin. It's not necessary." But that's not what I feel. My breast is part of me, and I am part of it. Where is my soul? Where are my feelings? Are they only in my heart? That is what everyone keeps telling me: they're in the heart. But is that true? How much of me is in my breast? Am I in every cell of my body?

How do people know my soul is not in my breast? That who I am is not there? Before they take my breast away, I want to move that part of who I am somewhere else, empty that part of my soul and myself into another part of my body.

Can I be whole without my breast? Can I make my peace with it? Writing as fast as I can, the words pour forth. I thank my breast. Thank it for what it has given me: for helping me recognize my transition from girlhood to womanhood, for nursing my babies and feeding them well, for giving me the shape and form of a woman. My breast pleased my husband, and it pleased me. Can I be whole without it?

All of a sudden, it is as if my breast is a separate being with a life of its own. As if it has plotted against me. I have taken care of it all these years and have taken such pride in it. I am angry at it for betraying me, for hosting this disease. Is it ready to go? Is that why this happened? Can I accept its desire to leave, like a child leaving a parent? I tell my parents they must let go of me. Am I ready to let go of my breast in the same way? To recognize it is time and let it go peacefully?

As I put the last words on the paper, I feel complete. I've mourned my breast, said thank you, and have moved the part of my soul that's in my breast to other parts of my body.

The sound of my family coming down the hall brings my attention back to this sterile room and my place in it. Hal, Dana, my parents, and everyone but Keaton all push through the doorway in a lump, all descending in a barrage of noise and chatter. In their wake, I'm almost relieved to see a stocky orderly pushing a stretcher. "Massie?" he says, "It's time."

"Yes, I'm ready. You see, it is now only skin."

Chapter Eight

*"I'm moving only clouds today; tomorrow,
I'll move mountains."*

After the mastectomy, my first awareness of the world around me is being in a hallway with my parents, husband, and daughter surrounding the gurney and staring down at me. Keaton hovers well out of reach, a few steps behind Hal and Dana. The soft skin around his brown eyes is creased in a way that makes him seem not eleven but eighty. A few steps behind my family, the faces of close friends come into focus. I feel like a dying patient being studied with great intent.

All eyes are on me when my mother, hands anchored tight at her breast, breaks the silence. "The doctor was just here, and everything went perfectly." I know my mother pretty well; even if I were in critical condition, she would tell me the same thing.

"Why do I have so many IVs in me?" The words stumble out as thick as my tongue feels. I can't believe so much effort is required to form a simple question. "Has the doctor said anything? Did they get all the cancer? Did he say something important like 'Close her up; we can't do anything for her'?" Everyone's eyes dart back and forth from one to the other but not to me. Obviously, they did not hear my question with the intended humor. "Well, did he say everything was okay?" Again, the darting eyes. "Okay, let's hear it. Why are you looking at each other like that?"

Dana, who stands closest to the gurney, is the only one gutsy enough to meet my eyes. She weaves her delicate fingers through mine. Fingers that have mastered the violin and cello well enough to play in

Portland's Youth Symphony yet tenacious enough to wield a mean varsity tennis racket. Tiny but mighty, her strength seeps through the warmth of her hand into mine and wills me to live.

After a moment of silence, Hal meets my eyes. "Lynne, the surgery took a lot longer than anticipated, and you lost a great deal of blood. After they removed the breast, they found another tumor down in your chest. Dr. Holmes is going to talk to us about it later when he gets all the pathology reports."

My mother jumps in. "But the doctor says you're going to be just fine." It sounds as if this sentence is a runaway train picking up speed with each word. By the time she gets to "be just fine," it sounds like one word, "bejustfine." Her hands begin to knead each other.

Another tumor? In my chest? This isn't part of the script. Dana holds my hand on one side and Hal on the other. They both squeeze, steady and strong.

In almost the same breath, my mother races on. "When they removed the breast and the lymph nodes, they took a look around to make sure they got everything. That's when they found the other tumor. It took them a while to get it out. The doctor's concerned, but Lynne, he has such faith in your determination."

Hal clears his throat and fiddles with his mechanical pencil. He looks lost without his yellow pad. "Lynne," he says, "what your mother's trying to say is that with the tumor in your chest, it means the cancer has spread. Dr. Holmes is worried and said the prognosis doesn't look good. However, he thinks you're a strong person, and if anyone can beat this, he's putting his money on you."

Leave it to Hal to cut to the point. In my groggy state, this news rolls right off me as if I, too, am standing with my family observing the steady drip of the IVs, the mumblings of this thick-tongued woman bedded in a crib of stainless steel and bleached white sheets. Apart from the dark brown hair framing her face, she's the picture of white on white, maybe near death. No connection to me. I'm very much alive. I have to be.

Mercifully, my eyes close, and just like that, Keaton's pained face and my mother's hand wringing and Hal's mechanical pencil are replaced by a piece of needlepoint on the wall of my laundry room. Stitched onto smooth white cloth are the words "I'm moving only clouds today; tomorrow, I'll move mountains." My mother gave me this quote for Christmas years ago and said that I was a master at taking things as they come. Perhaps that is one of the reasons I survived a life-threatening illness at sixteen and explains why I've done so well in life.

She's probably right. On the whole, I don't worry about what might be. I focus on whatever life hands me one piece at a time. Today, I can only recover from surgery. Tomorrow, I will move the mountain of survival. Cancer is not a death sentence, just another challenge to be taken as it comes. I am alive today, and I know I will be alive tomorrow. That is all I need to know for now. I have children to raise and a lot of living to do. I will simply have to fight harder than I first thought.

My hospital stay begins to feel like a marathon. One night has turned into four. The surgery was Monday, and on Thursday my blood pressure is still low. The vacuum pump connected to my surgical drain continues to fill with blood, and I'm still hooked up to two IVs. The nurses torture me by walking me up and down the hall every couple of hours, with IV poles rattling along beside me. All I want is to go home.

On Thursday afternoon, Dr. Holmes stands by my bed and debates whether to give me a transfusion. It's a sore subject. The week before the surgery, with the thought of a transfusion and the possibility of AIDS-tainted blood in mind, I asked whether I could donate a pint of my own blood. Dr. Holmes told me I wouldn't need a transfusion, that it was totally unnecessary. Now, he studies what must be a murderous look on my face and says, "We'll just give you more fluids and see how you are tomorrow."

On Friday, the news is good. Dr. Holmes says I get to go home, but I have to keep the drain in until I see him in his office the following week. A nurse steps in to show me how to care for it. The drain is constructed with a fairly long piece of plastic tubing about a quarter inch in diameter inserted into my chest. On the outer end of the tubing is a round vacuum pump device about six inches in diameter and about two inches high. The pump has a clip that holds it to the bed or my clothes.

My release is none too soon. Dana just graduated from eighth grade, and long before my stay at the Hospital Hilton, I ordered her a diamond and sapphire ring made from stones in a pin that had once belonged to her great aunt. Hal told me the jeweler called the other day to say the ring was ready. I'm eager to see it and hope it will become one of her family heirlooms. All I need to do is go to the mall tomorrow and pick it up.

But that is tomorrow. Today, Sheba and Snookers greet me as soon as I step into the house. Rear end wiggling, Sheba runs to her food bowl as if to say, "It's about time you came home to feed me."

I manage a feeble pat for both of them before the exhaustion of the car ride home sets in. No sooner do I crash in my own bed than Connie, a woman from the neighborhood, drops by to visit. She is an RN and a soccer mom. We always talk at the games, and I enjoy her immensely. But once off the soccer field, we have little or no contact. Occasionally, we wave as we drop our kids off at school or wheel down the aisles of the supermarket.

Connie enters my bedroom. "Hi, Lynne. I heard about your surgery from the neighbors, and I'm here to help. I can clean your drain and help you bathe these first few days." She leans over to give me a hug, and, with no warning, I burst into tears. What is this? I have been handling everything so well. I haven't cried in front of any of my friends and hardly at all in front of my family. Suddenly, I am totally dissolved in tears with this near stranger. My grief feels overwhelming. "I'm so sorry, Connie. I have no idea what came over me. I didn't mean to start crying."

But I can't stop crying or babbling. "I'm so scared. I didn't want to lose my breast. Now I don't know what's going to happen to me. I don't think I can do this anymore. I'm so tired of being positive and brave. What if I die? What if my kids have no mom? What are they going to do? Hal will be okay, but Dana and Keaton. How will they live without a mom watching them play soccer, helping them with their homework, cooking their favorite meals, making stupid Halloween costumes? Help me, Connie. Help me cope."

With a nurse's smile, she says, "I will. I'm right down the street, and I'll be here every day. Now let's get that drain cleaned so you can get some rest." I fall back into my pillows and am so grateful she is here. Wow, talk about letting people in and making changes.

I still have pain, a lot of pain. Moving my arm is impossible and just taking a deep breath causes pain around the opening for the drain. Crashing in my own bed feels like I have gone to heaven. After a long nap, I wake with my mother standing at my side. She has a pain pill in one hand and a glass of water in the other. "I'm not taking any pain pills," I say. "Aspirin will do just fine. That's all I want."

"Lynne, if you didn't need these pills, the doctor wouldn't have prescribed them. Besides, the pain will just wear you down." This begins a family argument. I am so afraid I'm going to die. I'm so afraid that if I take pain pills, I will mentally lose some of the minutes I have left. My body screams out to stop the pain, and my brain tells me to cope with it because pain may become my way of life. I don't know when the road I'm traveling will turn away from those I love, when I'll have to get off this train called "life." What I do know is that I don't want to miss a moment of it. I would rather sit by the window in pain and look at the sun than drift aimlessly in and out of a pain-free sleep.

Rather than take narcotics, I use simple aspirin. Then in the quiet hours, I put on soft music and beg my pain to go away, to stop hammering at me. Through meditation, I cajole it into becoming a friend, a friend that reminds me to listen to my body. I promise the pain that if it will just subside to a dull ache, I'll listen and remember to take care of myself. Music and meditation ease my mind's focus on the pain and let it drift to more pleasant places while I heal.

In spite of my peace with my decision, it seems that those who have no pain have a lot to say about those who are in pain. My family thinks I should see a psychiatrist. They think my refusal to give in to the drugs is some kind of masochistic tendency that will only exacerbate if left untreated. I don't see how they can fail to understand what makes perfect sense to me. Pain pills are for those who think they have a long time to live. People in acute pain can take a pill, dull the pain, and be knocked out for an hour or two and still know that they will once again enjoy life. The grogginess from the pills and the cotton in their brains will clear, leaving them free to go on about their lives. Chronic pain coupled with pain pills could easily become a way of life—my way of life—because this pain may never go away. I want to keep my mind as clear as possible. Besides, I have to get that ring for Dana, and I can't go to the mall while I'm drugged with pain medication.

On Saturday, the day after I came home from the hospital, I struggle out of bed and announce that I want someone to take me to the mall to get Dana's ring. Six pairs of eyes and three open mouths are my response. My family is now convinced I am certifiably crazy.

"You can't go to the mall," my mother says. "Did your doctor say you could do this?"

In my most logical tone of voice, I respond, "They made me walk around the halls of the hospital. I can't see that the mall is any different. My doctor didn't tell me I couldn't go to the mall. I just need someone to help me get dressed and drive me there."

Leaving the room, I hear muttering. "It probably never occurred to him that you would try."

Reluctantly, my father volunteers to do the driving against protests from my mother, who now sees him as a coconspirator. Hal throws up his hands and says, "Hey, it is up to her. If she feels like going to the mall, that's okay. Once she has made up her mind, whatever she wants to happen happens." Watching me struggle to dress with the use of only one arm, my mother decides to help me while muttering under her breath the entire time. "You shouldn't be doing this. I think you're nuts."

My father and I are soon off to the mall. Whizzing down the freeway, I am a happy camper and am amazed at how different the scenery looks. Scenery marked for years as a blur in my peripheral vision sharpens into blades of grass, a broken fence, the cliff at High Rocks. Everything is sharper, alive, and more intense.

My father drops me off at the door to the mall, and as I begin walking, I discover one tiny problem. The clip that is supposed to hold the pump to my shirt keeps slipping. The drain and the pump, both hidden under my shirt, keep coming loose and falling down. The tubing attached to the pump is not quite long enough to reach the floor.

So when the pump comes loose, it acts like a yo-yo. It drops about two inches from the floor before it reaches the end of its tubing with a jerk and then bounces back up again. This happens about every ten feet. To say "ouch" would be putting it mildly.

By the time I make it to the jewelry store, I have one hand over the pump near my missing breast to keep it from slipping. I can't wait to see my doctor next week. He is going to hear about this drain problem.

People stare as I walk into the elegant jewelry store, surely noting the rumpled clothes, the hair that has been combed but remains out of control. Then there is the inward roll of my shoulders and the slight unsteadiness of my gait. The clerks and other customers look at me as if I've just left skid row and have come to rob the place. Noses wrinkle in anticipation of a bad smell. Even though I bathed, people just assume I'll have an odor. I look a far cry from the sophisticated businesswoman who spends a lot of time and energy on grooming and dressing.

Even the store's owner, who met me twice before, can hardly believe his eyes. However, he knows I have been in the hospital and, like the gentleman he is, takes this all in stride. He hands me the ring, which is stunning, and my father drives me back home.

The following week, Hal and I are in the room with the view that overlooks the Willamette River. On the far side of the river, the wooded ridge still stands untouched. This view has become such an integral part of my journey–a touchstone in the face of change.

Dr. Holmes hardly makes it through the door before I start in on the drain. "I have a complaint about this thing. The tubing is too short. You should have seen me at the mall on Saturday. It kept falling off. You should modify your technique and make the tubing three inches longer than the height of the patient," I say. "Then the pump will stay on the floor and not bounce up again. Should I write instructions for you?"

"You don't understand," he says, chuckling and eyeing me over his half-glasses. "My technique is to measure the distance to the bottom of your feet and subtract three inches. That way when the drain falls off and jerks the tubing, it reminds you to go home and get back in bed! I never imagined you would try to go to the mall. However, with you, I should have known better. I was going to tell you today that you could start being more active, but it looks like that is no longer necessary."

After we share a good laugh, he hits me with the bad news. The entire breast was malignant along with all the other surrounding tissue they took out. They were hoping to find a point where there were noncancerous cells. However, this was not the case. The cancer appears to have spread to my chest. I glanced at the open chart and saw he had written "fifty-one year old with poor prognosis."

"Lynne," he says, "I know this doesn't sound good, and I can't tell you the outcome of this. I see cancer patients who statistically shouldn't make it more than a few months who are alive and kicking ten years later. Then I see others who statistically have every reason in the world to look forward to a long, healthy life, and they die in six months. We doctors can do just so much, and then some other force takes over." Shaking his head, he looks down at his feet and says, "I can't explain it."

As the days go on, my physical pain gives way to emotional pain and determination. Pain becomes my friend and reminds me to fight. I will not dull it any more than absolutely necessary. Pain reminds me that I must see the flowers, stand tall in the sunlight, and keep my brain intact.

Chapter Nine

*I want to know that I have done
everything possible to survive.*

omorrow, the chemotherapy treatments start. I am
not ready for them. Chemotherapy represents a
change that I am not sure I want. A change in how
I work and live. A change that will affect my career and my family. It
means slowing down, a new lifestyle, a new way of eating, drinking,
waking, and sleeping.

Change. It's only a word to most people. It isn't their life, their
essence, their soul that has to make the sacrifice. It is mine, and I have
no choice. In order to survive I have to change. I have to learn to eat
differently, work differently, exercise more than my mind. How in the
world am I going to suddenly change everything about me, the essence
of who I am? I am in all things I do. Fast, slow, eating, sleeping,
drinking. It is all me. Can I become someone else?

Growing up, change was exciting. It was the fun part of life. The
anticipation of kindergarten: "When Mommy? Huh? When can I go to
school?" Then middle school: "Oh, boy, I'm really growing up now. Hot
diggity." High school: "It can't get any better than this. This is really
groovy. I can't wait until I can drive." College: "You mean it's possible to
change even beyond this? No way, this is the ultimate. This is the best."
Change was happy, anticipated, and fun.

Now change is suddenly the enemy. I didn't ask for it and am not
at all sure I can cope with it. I love who I am and who I have been: the
successful career woman with two healthy and well-adjusted children

and a supportive husband. I love my busy life. Will survival be worth the slow down, the change in diet, the change in my family dynamics? Who will I become? My name will still be Lynne, but will I still be Lynne? What if I don't even recognize myself when I am well? Will I get into bed at night and wonder "Where is Lynne?"

There is the possibility that I could become a better me and like myself better. Maybe even others will like me better. However, some of my treasured friends and family may not like the new me at all. That is what scares me: that I'll lose people I love, that my change will start a chain reaction that will be as uncomfortable and unwelcome for them as it is for me. I am afraid that rather than face that discomfort, some of my friends and family will drift away. First, there will be the long stares as they scrutinize my changing appearance. Then will come the awkward pauses in conversation as they catch themselves about to refer to something we may have had in common in the past. They'll check their watch once too often during our visit and end by saying, "We really need to get together more often"; but then never call.

In my attempt to stay alive, what if I hate who I become? Once I am well, can I hit the rewind button and go back to the way things were without causing a recurrence of my cancer?

Well-meaning friends and family tell me I have to change to get well, but they do not understand what that means. From the moment of my diagnosis, those around me have behaved as if I was not capable of taking care of myself. Unsolicited advice comes from everywhere. "Do this, do that, work fewer hours, take more naps, eat different foods, meditate." I didn't feel any need to change yesterday. Why should I feel the need to change today?

I've been reading loaned books on meditation. There are as many types of meditation as there are spaghetti sauces: Simple Seated, Walking, Transcendental, Mindfulness, Vibrational, Body Scan, Taoist, Microcosmic Orbit, and last, but not least, Breath and Navel Meditation. Do I hum, chant, or focus on a mantra or my navel? The first time I tried meditation, I sat quietly to witness whatever went through my mind without attachment to thought or worry or images, but I got impatient, and then angry, when nothing happened. To get angry and frustrated at what is supposed to take away your anger doesn't seem like a good change. Giving up was tempting, but failing felt worse, so I told myself to try again. "Okay, Lynne, calm yourself. You can do this. Meditate. Breathe in. Breathe out. Slow down. Let the anger dissipate."

Good intentions aside, the endless advice from friends, family, and mere acquaintances is overwhelming. Why people feel they have the right to step into my life and start giving mandates is beyond me. These friends, family, and near strangers point out how stressful and busy my life has been and how jet lag has led to my disease. Over and over I hear, "Stress has to be the cause of your cancer." These words of wisdom are not from medical professionals but self-appointed advisors. Another one I often hear is "You have too much fat in your diet. High fat causes breast cancer." But how high is too high? My doctors don't know the answer, yet these people are convinced my eating and working habits are the cause.

The unspoken message is that I have somehow caused this disease. Guilt overwhelms me. Could I have prevented it? Which part of my life was the culprit? The travel, lack of exercise, my dashboard diet? How much of what do I have to give up to survive? Do I have to give up my entire way of life to survive? Or can I give up only a portion of it? Which part?

It's so odd to have the tables turned, to go from being considered the person who can handle anything and everything that comes along to the person who supposedly can't even feed herself properly. Always, people have asked me for advice, oftentimes people I hardly know. I am used to being the one who gives advice, not the one who receives it. Why should cancer change my standing in the world? Why should my credibility be undermined because this insidious disease has chosen me as its host?

Do these self-appointed advisors know what their advice means? These are only words to them. This isn't their life. It isn't their essence. Their souls don't have to change and make the sacrifices. I do, and I have no choice.

Soon, all of the pathology results from the mastectomy are in. I anxiously sit in my oncologist's office and notice silver-gray streaks through dark hair that is pulled back at the nape of her neck. She wears no makeup, not even lipstick, on her narrow face. Somehow this unmasked intensity lends her words heightened credibility.

"Lynne, your cancer is aggressive. We have two choices. Your first treatment option is a very aggressive program that will be difficult, but it has the potential of preventing the cancer from ever returning. If we go with this, you'll be given your lifetime maximum of the drugs. With the drugs we now have, should the cancer return, your options will be limited."

I wish I were in Dr. Holmes's office, where I could anchor my sanity on that unbroken ridge of pines above the Willamette River.

"The other choice we have right now is a slightly milder program, although still fairly aggressive. The advantage of this program is that it will allow us to hold the most aggressive drugs in reserve in the event of a recurrence."

This is a no-brainer. To sit back and not take the most aggressive approach is completely against my nature. "I have to know I've done everything possible," I say. "I'll deal with a recurrence when and if it happens. Who knows, maybe some new wonder drug will have been developed. In the meantime, give it all you've got."

"Okay," she says. "We'll begin on Wednesday."

Wednesday's approach finds me terrified. I'm frightened about what will happen to me when I step through this threshold of change. I will never again be the same. I will never come back to my life as it was before cancer. I'm groping for something solid where there is only air. I have always believed change takes on different characteristics. Some change comes and goes and is easily reversed. Then there is change that moves only in one direction, never to be reversed.

The feeling is reminiscent of when Keaton was eight and went off to camp for the first time. In the parking lot, we clung to each other while waiting for the busses to fill. I was excited for Keaton yet afraid he would be homesick, afraid he might not make friends, but mostly afraid of letting go.

Several days later, I stood in the same parking lot and waited to pick him up after his week at camp. The voices of happy campers could be heard loud and clear belting out camp songs as the bus rounded the corner. Tears welled in my eyes as I pictured the homecoming–my little boy so glad to be home as he leaped off the bus and into my arms.

The bus door opened, and campers spilled out onto the parking lot. When Keaton finally stepped down, he took one look at me, waved, and said "Hi, Mom." No running into my arms, no hugs, just a casual acknowledgment before turning to his new friends to make sure he had their phone numbers. I smiled and reminded myself that as little boys grow up, mothers recede into the background. This is the way it is meant to be: life moving irreversibly forward, one instant, one experience, changing things forever. Keaton had just stepped through a major threshold of change, never to step back again.

It's been a long day. Tomorrow it starts. The chemotherapy and the change begin. The terror of the chemotherapy looms. I'd give anything to avoid this. Each nightly ritual becomes overshadowed by uneasiness. Eating supper, I catch myself thinking that it is my last supper before–before what? What effect is chemotherapy going to have on me? Later, the rhythm of my tooth brushing is interrupted by the thought that this is the last time I brush my teeth as the Lynne I know. Closing my eyes to let the thoughts dissipate has no effect. I can't seem to stem the flow of my mind's speculation. I never expected the mastectomy to change anything other than the physical me. It didn't scare me. It is the chemo that frightens me. My gut says it will change me forever. Am I teetering at the beginning of my end? In bed, I pray, · "Please, God, more time. Please give me more time before this begins."

Even though intellectually I know my doctors are right, I'd still give anything for them to call and say they made a mistake, that it isn't me they are supposed to treat. That night I dream I am standing on the end of a thirty-meter diving board with my toes hanging over the edge. I'm trying to get up the courage to jump into the icy water below. The sensation of free-falling, of being out of control and unable to stop, jolts me awake. The sight of Hal on the other side of the bed gives me reassurance.

As I look at the phone on the bedside table, I know that I can pick up that receiver in the morning and say, "No. I'm not going to do this." I have the control and the power, yet the illusion is flimsy. Survival leaves me no choice. Undergoing chemotherapy is the only option. I want to live, and I want to know that I have done everything possible to survive.

Tomorrow the change begins. I will try really hard to do what I am supposed to do. As I drift back to sleep, the phone is silent. I know without a doubt that it is I who must be ready. No one else can do it for me. It is I who must endure this. I want to live. I want to survive. I must be ready, when the alarm blares in the morning, to walk into that hospital and step through the threshold of change.

Chapter Ten

I'll never eat creamed eggs again.

As Hal and I pull out of the driveway for the hospital the next morning, I feel as if I am going to the guillotine. On my last visit to the oncologist, I asked her why I needed to be admitted to the hospital for the treatments. Most of her patients have their chemo in her office. In my case, she said the drugs are so toxic they have to be administered intravenously, under closer supervision than they can provide in her office. The word "toxic" loops through my head over and over.

I enter the outpatient door of the hospital on legs shaking from fear. It has been only six weeks since my mastectomy, and the corridors look all too familiar. Hal surrenders me to the admitting desk, pecks my cheek, and says he'll catch up with me in the treatment room after he finds a parking place in the overcrowded lot.

Sitting in a too-low chair across from the admitting clerk who is collecting personal information, I find my voice is surprisingly steady. Nothing in the clerk's manner recognizes the fact that I could be dead in a year or that checking in for the first of what will be months of chemotherapy treatments is anything out of the ordinary. I try to mirror her nonchalant attitude, act as if this is no big deal, but when she secures the name band on my wrist, the quiver of my fingers gives me away.

Only a few other times in my life have I shaken from fear, the most recent being five years ago when the company I was working for was involved in a make-or-break lawsuit. I had to testify at a deposition. I practiced my name all the way to the courthouse and kept telling myself that I couldn't do this court stuff. I was too afraid. They would hear the fear in my voice, think I was covering something up instead of just being nervous, and my deposition would be the one to drag the entire company under. In the moment before the court reporter took my name, the words of my psychologist friend came back to me. "Lynne, you can be scared, and you can do it. One does not preclude the other."

Walking down the corridors of the hospital, I hear those words ringing in my ears once again. I can be afraid, and I can do this. I am doing it. One foot in front of the other, moving down the hall, not dropping dead. I make it all the way to the nurses' station, where a middle-aged nurse with a very prominent nose directs me to the room where the treatment will occur. Instead of just walking right in, I stick out my neck and peek through the door. To my surprise, it is a regular hospital room furnished with several recliners instead of beds. IV poles loom behind each chair, and a television is mounted near the ceiling. Against the wall is a bookcase with video tapes and books. Beside each chair is a small basket of cookies. I inch into the room and half expect monsters to leap out of the closet.

No sooner do I settle into one of the recliners, eye the cookies, and think this might not be so bad than the nurse is back with a basket containing several plastic IV bags. On go her rubber gloves and then an extra pair of very long gloves stretching up to her elbows, a special rubber apron, mask, and goggles. My mind starts racing. "What's happening here? Why are you wearing all this stuff?" I ask. "This looks like a science fiction movie."

"These drugs are very corrosive, and we have to be careful not to get any on our skin."

Oh, great. That's reassuring. They're going inside of me! Once the IV is hooked up, the nurse begins the drip of the anti-nausea drug. She explains that it is fast acting, so I won't get sick when she gives me the other drugs. I try not to focus on the ache as the cool liquid flows into my arm. Instead, I focus on her nose, the bump on the bridge, the way it sits crooked on her face.

Once she is satisfied with the IV's progress, the nurse leaves me to idle. Nothing is on television, so I thumb through a few magazine pages but find my gaze catching on the IV's slow drip. As Hal arrives in the treatment room, doubt worms its way to the surface of my thoughts and stirs up fear. Panic is close. I suck in one deep breath, then another, and hope my previous rantings haven't excommunicated me from God altogether. I offer up a quick prayer that the anti-nausea drug works as Hal takes my hand.

Once the IV is empty, I receive Adriomycin, the most potent of the cancer-fighting drugs. This is the one that is going to make my hair fall out. After an interminable wait, the bag empties, and the nurse hooks up another one containing Cytoxin, the drug that causes most of the nausea.

"Why do people get nauseated?" I ask the nurse. The answer is the same reason people lose their hair. The drugs are designed to attack rapidly growing cells. Cancer cells, hair follicles, and cells lining the stomach are all fast-growing cells. The drugs can't distinguish the difference. They kill all three.

The final drug is Fluorouracil (5-FU). As the 5-FU enters my body, the words in the magazine I've been pretending to read begin to blur. "Is this normal?" I ask, the panic in my voice unmasked. "Am I going to lose my vision?" Even the nurse's nose is unfocused.

The nurse assures me this blurring is a normal side effect. She probably thinks I belong in the loony bin instead of the treatment room.

Four long hours later, treatment number one is behind me. The nurse instructs me to drink lots of water to flush the drugs from my kidneys. "Your urine will turn red," she says, "from the Adriomycin, so don't be alarmed."

Don't be alarmed? I feel I am in a vortex. One day I am an international marketing specialist who flies all over the world, and the next my doctors tell me I can't work so many hours. I have to slow down. Twenty hours a week, not sixty. Suddenly–poof–my career is not the same. One day I am eating at the local fast food spot or in a gourmet French restaurant in Paris, and the next well-meaning friends tell me I should be eating tofu and fat-free skinless chicken, that I should exercise and meditate. Suddenly–poof–my body belongs to others.

I resent the fact that my life is changing so fast while others go blissfully about their daily lives. Yet I realize that if I am to survive, my daily wants no longer matter. My choices are change or certain death, so I have to adjust whether I want to or not. This is not like my children's graduations, or vacations, or retirement where I have time to plan, where I can decide, yes, I'll take the cancer or no, I'll pass. This disease hit me broadside, without warning, right in the middle of a perfectly satisfactory life. I didn't ask for it. It just occurred. In one day–boom. No warning.

To my dismay, my immediate family and friends seem happy about the change. The kids and Hal love me being home for them instead of at the office or jet-setting all over the world. My friends are happy to spend time visiting and helping me. Even Sheba loves the more frequent walks. But what about me? I don't know whether I can adjust. I hate all this change. Yet I want to live, so I feel I have no choice but to embrace it. But I will not give up my right to be alarmed. Amen. And, Hal, help me out of this damn recliner.

Hal walks me from the hospital to the car after this first day of chemotherapy. He sticks close, a hand under my elbow to guide me. "How you doing, Lynne?"

What have these drugs done to my brain? I hear his words coming at me as if through two tin cans connected by string. I hear my answers, too, but they don't make sense. My legs hear the message from my brain to keep moving, but it's as if the message is coming from someone else's brain. Minute by minute, my body feels more and more disconnected. My legs are slack, rubbery like those on a puppet.

It is a good thing my family didn't listen to my insistence that I could drive myself to and from the treatments! I don't think I could see the other cars or even the road at this point. I hate this feeling. It's frightening. For someone who has lived most of her life by handling situations without fear, it seems to be hitting me smack dab in the face at every turn.

Thankfully, the kids are still at school when Hal and I arrive home. He is close to my side, ready to steady me should my legs give way. Sheba greets me first, her nose glued to my IV arm as I reach out to pet her. Following a long examination with much sniffing, she shakes her head hard and then rubs her big nose against my pant leg. "I know," I tell her, my voice echoing in my head. "I wish I could shake it off, too." My mother flutters around me and mutters about something to eat, something light of course. "Maybe creamed eggs, Lynne. You love those."

Last week, my oncologist warned me not to eat any of my favorite foods after the treatment. I had a good breakfast and haven't thought about food since. Creamed eggs over toast sound fabulous. They go down easily, taste great, and, besides, I have certainly earned something good. I feel pretty good, and I'm hungry. I decide to forget what the oncologist said. I want creamed eggs.

Elbows propped on the kitchen table, I watch my mother bustle around the kitchen, a bit blurry like that magazine at the hospital. My father pushes through the kitchen door with an armload from the grocery store, everything my mother thinks a sick person needs: eggs, black tea, bread for toast, saltines, ginger ale, orange juice, popsicles, some sort of high-protein liquid food supplement. On top of the bag is a package of raw liver that I silently vow not to touch. My mother read that people on chemo need lots of iron, so liver was prominent on her grocery list. Gag. No thank you.

The phone rings the moment my mother puts my creamed eggs down in front of me. My parents and I look at each other for the first few rings and wait for someone to take action. Finally, my mother tells my father to make himself useful and answer the phone. It is the office. Convinced they cannot function without me, I told my staff they could call me at home anytime, so I am not surprised to find my coworker Lea on the line.

Lea proceeds to ask me a fairly involved question about the new product release, and to my dismay, I am completely blank. I have no understanding of what she is talking about. Here I sit unable to discuss something I've been involved in since the get-go. I can't believe I am unable to discuss the company's most important project. It's like forgetting the name of one of my kids. Finally, I tell her we should talk in a few days, and I let the receiver drift toward its cradle. Weird, very weird.

For some thirty hours after the treatment, I lie in bed and am unable to concentrate on reading or television. I wake from intermittent dozing to find Dana or my mother always at the end of my bed. Dana is respectful of my silences, my lapses in conversation, whereas my mother construes each hiccup as a sure indication of further decline. During these long hours, I sip water and wear a path in the carpet to and from the bathroom. I wait to feel better or at least different.

"Different" hits with a thunderbolt of uncontrollable vomiting. So much for the anti-nausea medication. All I can think of are creamed eggs. The vomiting continues for what seems like hours. My oncologist tells me to go back to the hospital for a different nausea medication and assures me we will find something that works. "We don't want you sick. We want to make this experience as pleasant as possible." Pleasant? She has to be kidding.

Hunched over a basin in my lap on the way to the hospital, I vow I'll never eat creamed eggs again.

For the next three days, the thought of food sends me running for the bathroom. I can eat nothing without getting sick, and not eating causes a big ruckus between me and my mother. "You'll starve to death before the cancer kills you," she says. "Please, please eat something."

"Have you ever tried to eat while you're nauseated, Mother? It's impossible." My mother, dear mother. Only staying with us for a short time and wanting so much to care for me through this ordeal. The constant tension has put even Sheba off her food. This Mt. Everest of the animal kingdom noses through her kibble and then pads over to stand at my side. Panting lightly, she leans into my leg and nudges her nose under my hand until I stroke the top of her head.

"Lynne, I am so worried about you." Mother again. The hair on the back of my neck rises at her high pitched do-as-I-say whine. "Daddy and I just want the best for you."

Whenever my mother thinks she is losing an argument, she drags my father into the picture, as if big, powerful Daddy supports her every opinion. What my mother fails to understand is that her idea of what is best for me and my idea of what is best for me are sometimes quite different.

The next few days unravel like this: my mother trying to get me to eat and me gagging at every offering. At noon on the third day, she comes at me again, this time with an orange juice/raw egg concoction. Surely this is a joke. "Mother, I am not going to drink this. It's disgusting. I'm calling my doctor, and if she says I don't have to eat, I'm not eating."

It's Saturday, and I hate bothering my doctor at home, but this is war. My doctor's main concern is my getting enough water. However, my mother is still not convinced, and out come the liquid food supplements. She begs me to drink one instead of the orange juice with the raw egg. Worn down, I take a tentative sip. The artificial vanilla is too sweet, too thick, too much like a liquid antacid. I gag it down just to make peace, thankful that my parents' departure is on the near horizon.

Of course, my mother does not want to leave. She is worried that with six months of chemotherapy ahead of me, I am going to crumble and drop dead any minute. I understand her fear, but her continuous presence is a barrier between me and my own family. As long as my mother is taking care of me and hovering around, the kids and Hal stay more or less in the background. One afternoon I find myself telling her, "Mother, you and Daddy have to leave. You can't stay for six months or a year or however long this takes. In spite of all your caretaking, I'm still sick, and you're not going to single-handedly change that. We need to get our lives back as close to normal as possible."

The misty-eyed hand wringing is in full swing, the silence thick, broken only by my mother's faint whisper. "I just don't want the next time I see you to be on your death bed."

Chapter Eleven

"Why did my Mom have to get this?"

A week later, with tears all around, my parents fly back to Atlanta. My family and I are now faced with each other and the inconvenience of cancer. Getting the laundry, the shopping, and the after-school junkets to music and sports done is a challenge. I'm guessing the kids and Hal thought that once my parents left, I'd rise from my sick bed and resume life as we all know it, but I still feel sick from my first treatment and continue to lie in bed most of the day. I sip water and drag myself no further than the bathroom and back.

No one says anything for the first week. Hal proceeds as usual, not noticing the ever-growing pile of laundry and dishes accumulating on the kitchen counter. These things have never been part of Hal's universe, and I'm not sure he sees them now.

Keaton keeps to his room except when Hal rouses him out before bed to say good night to me. When I ask him about how things are going at school, I get more mumbling than answers. I know he is really scared. I think his fear of my cancer is even worse than that of my plane crashing like the space shuttle.

The other day, he came home from school with a poem he had written. He called it "I'm Sad."

I don't understand. Why did my mom have to get this?
Why did cancer have to become a case?
Why do I feel so guilty as if I caused it to happen?
Why do I feel like I need to do something to help her get well?

Why is it that whenever I see her lying there in the hospital or think of her, I cry?

Why can't I share my feelings about this with other people besides her?

Why can't I just forget about this and move on?

Why do I feel like I am in a cage and can't get out?

Dana, on the other hand, in her "tiny but mighty" way, rallies and rises earlier in the morning to fix breakfast for herself and Keaton. She tends to Sheba and Snookers and sits at the end of my bed in the afternoons while I doze. Sometimes we talk. For that first week, I can hardly string two thoughts together, so it is mostly Dana describing the day outside or who is doing what at school. Then one afternoon, when she has arrived home to find that the ice cream is melting on the counter and that her brother hasn't let the dogs out in time to avoid some very unpleasant cleanup, her conversation takes a turn. "Mom, this is twisted! You're supposed to go to the hospital to get better. You went in sick and came home worse. I always thought that sickness stayed in the hospital. I was wrong. This disease has taken over our whole family. It didn't evaporate in the car when you came home. It's like we've all been thrown into a clothes dryer, tumbled around, and then told to walk straight. It's impossible. Keaton's having trouble in school, I sit in class all day worrying about you, and Dad has to go to work every day. This is so dumb. Keaton wrote a poem, and so did I. I called mine 'Anger.'"

Anger is when your best friend betrays you.

Anger is when someone you care about dies in a car accident.

Anger is when your dog dies.

Anger is when someone you love is in pain.

Anger is when your mom has cancer.

Anger is when your parents yell at you.

Anger is when you hear a door slam or a foot stomp.

Anger is when you flunk a test or get a bad grade.

Anger is when you know you're right and no one will listen.

Anger is the question "Why?"

Dana's vehemence has me fully alert for the first time since the chemo. I'm chagrined. I realize we are all arguing over everyday things: laundry, cooking, and cleaning. This leaves me feeling as though I have failed my family.

Several days later, my friend Lee stops by to check on me. Having been through the long months of hell preceding his son's death from AIDS, Lee understands the stress of long-term illness on a family. I bemoan the struggle cancer is causing, the fact that my life is changing at breakneck speed, that my family and friends seem happy about my slowdown but simultaneously frustrated when expectations built on a relationship with the old me no longer apply. I vacillate between rage, fear, and grief for a lost way of life.

Lee mostly listens and cracks a joke where he can squeeze one in. Then he listens to me complain. I tell him that resentment has mounted over the fact that my life has flipped upside down rapidly while others go blissfully about their daily lives as they have always done. I hate the speed with which change is occurring. I know that if I am to survive, daily wants and desires no longer matter. Often I lie in bed at night and scream at God. "I can't do this. Why are you doing this to me?" I go on to tell Lee that my mother told me God gives people only what they can handle. "Well, I've got news for God. This is beyond my limit. I am not trying to build character. I am trying to survive. I only want the strength to get through this and make certain I live."

After quietly listening to my frustration, he scribbles a phone number on a piece of scratch paper and places it gently in my hand. "His name is Nick," he says. "He's a hospice counselor. Stop trying to do this alone, and call him. Take Hal and the kids so you can deal with this as a family instead of just knocking heads."

Nick is about forty, with a small build, a beard, and kind, twinkling eyes. His office is warm and friendly with soft lamplight, a dream catcher, a child's framed artwork, and a soft, comfortable couch. The kids should be okay here when we bring them.

Hal and I take the sofa, and Nick ignores the executive chair behind the desk and instead opts for a deep leather chair across from the couch. We hardly finish the pleasantries before I start crying to him the way I cry to God. "What if I die? How do we hold the family together? What will they do without me? Help me. Help us. This is your job. We need you to manage this process. We can't do it by ourselves. I think Hal is taking it too lightly. He just keeps throwing statistics at me and doesn't seem to grasp the fact that I may die. He just keeps saying I'll be okay when I may not be."

Ankle crossed over knee, Nick inclines his head in a silent nod. His eyes lock onto mine in a way that invites me to continue. "Hal just ignores this whole thing as if I have a cold. Whenever I try to talk about being scared or dying, he cuts me off with his stupid statistics. Could you please tell him he has to stop acting as if this is no big deal, as if I just have a bad cold?"

Again Nick nods and glances at Hal in a way that I interpret as disapproving. So I am taken aback when Nick says, "Lynne, every person deals with cancer in a different way. You, being the patient, have somewhat of an advantage."

The hinge of my jaw goes slack. Advantage? Is this guy crazy?

Nick leans forward. "You know at every minute how you feel inside. To others, you look the same outside no matter how sick you are inside. Hal is scared, too. He just lost his mother, and now he thinks he may lose his wife. I'm sure it's overwhelming him. I'm not saying you have to like the way he's behaving, but it is the way he copes. You've seen this before in other situations. After twenty years of marriage, you know his reaction to stress. Isn't this how he handled his mother's death? By just ignoring it?"

"I just wish Hal could be different," I say. "I want him to step into this change with me so he will know what it's all about and understand this part of my life. If he were to talk about how he feels, I think it would help our son, Keaton, deal with his feelings. But with Hal not willing to talk about anything he considers nonlinear, how can he help the kids? Change is being forced on me so fast. I want him to have to change, too."

Nick does not move a muscle. Even now his steady gaze meets mine, on hold, waiting. I want to reach forward and shake him. I want a response. Finally, when Nick is satisfied that I'm done, he asks, "Do you think it's really possible that you're the only one changing?"

"Well, maybe not. But I don't know what's happening with the others. They don't tell me, and I am not sure they know, either."

We depart Nick's with at least a little bit more awareness of what is happening in the family. Next time the kids will come with us.

At home, we fall into a routine, and the help we hire lowers the family stress level enough so that I can concentrate on important things such as my impending hair loss. The week before my first chemotherapy treatment, my mother and I spent hours in a local wig shop–fitting, cutting, trimming–making certain I would look just the same after my hair loss as before. By the time we left the shop, we were both convinced no one would be able to tell the difference.

For many years, how I looked or dressed or what kind of car I drove had to meet the approval of the entire population. So, of course, it never occurred to me to go wigless when I went bald. Not only would I wear a wig, but I would also be prepared the moment my hair fell out. The wig would be slapped on, and I would look like I am supposed to look: prim, proper, and well-groomed. I am ready.

Yesterday, I asked my doctor about the hair loss. "Will it come out in clumps? One clump one day on the right side and another clump the next day on the left? Will I shed like a dog? What is it going to be like?"

"Sudden," she said. "About ten to fourteen days after your first chemotherapy treatment."

Each morning, I have marked the days. One, two, three. Day ten arrives, and nothing happens. Day eleven. Nothing. Maybe I will be the exception, and my hair won't fall out after all. On day twelve, my head begins to itch. Gently, I tug at my hair. No, not yet. My hair is still very well attached to my head.

On day thirteen, my scalp hurts. It doesn't hurt on the inside like a headache. It hurts on the outside as if I have combed my hair in the wrong direction. It hurts so much I have to scrunch up my pillow under my neck to keep my head suspended so my hair does not touch anything. Yet, when I tug once again, the hair is still firmly rooted to my scalp.

Day fourteen. I wake up and tug at my hair. Nothing. Still firmly implanted in my head. But I notice something different this morning.

The itching is much worse, like a severe case of head lice. Maybe if I take a shower and shampoo my hair, it will feel better. I step into the shower, begin to scrub my hair, and sigh with relief. It feels sooooo good. But when I take my hands away, masses of hair are webbed between my fingers. "Yikes!" I shriek at the hair cascading down my body. I look like a gorilla taking a shower. As I continue massaging my scalp, hair comes out by the handfuls and clogs the drain. The bottom of the shower is ankle deep in water, and as I lean over to scoop up the hair, my tears begin to drip into the swirling water.

Stepping out of the shower, I don't quite have the courage to look in the mirror, so I side step to the trash can. But there is no avoiding the moment. A very quick glance into the mirror, over my shoulder, tells me I can no longer pretend that I don't have this disease. I suck in a deep breath and turn to face myself. About ninety-five percent of my hair is gone. The five percent left is scattered about my head unevenly in wisps and tufts. Somehow I had pictured my head slick and shiny, not goofy like this.

The kids are in school, Hal is at work, and I am alone in the house. Both excitement and sadness overwhelm me, an odd mixture of pain and joy. I lift my wig out of the dresser drawer, slip it on, and slowly turn to the mirror for the final adjustments. I tweak and tug on my new hair for what must be close to half an hour. Although the wig duplicates my pre-cancer look perfectly, it feels like a hat perched on top of my head. It sure doesn't feel a part of me.

When I bought the wig, the saleswoman also tried to sell me scarves and turbans. "You'll want something casual for when you do the laundry," she said. "Something to wear around the house." Yuk, no way. I will conform to the world and wear the wig when I am out of my house, but I am not going to wear anything on my head in my own home. Forget it.

Throughout the day, I occasionally catch sight of my bald head in the mirror. The first few times, the image startles me, but by early afternoon, I am very nearly comfortable with the Lynne staring back, and I am comfortable enough to settle at my desk and lose myself in work.

By the time I surface several hours later, my thirst is raging, and the refrigerator is empty. No soft drinks, no iced tea, nothing. So I do what I always do. I grab my purse and drive to the store. In the parking lot, I look into the rearview mirror and suddenly realize my wig is at home. Yikes! Do I go home and get it, or do I take a chance no one will see me? I am tired. I don't feel well. At this point, I am not sure I care what the world thinks. Besides, I'll be in the store only a few minutes. If I see someone I know, I can duck down another aisle before they see me. I'll be in and out in a flash, like streaking to the linen closet after my shower for a fresh towel.

I dash across the parking lot, and then the soft swish of the supermarket doors brings me face to face with a seventeen-year-old girl toting a sparse bag of groceries. Her jeans sport large tears. Studs and earrings perforate her eyebrows, ears, nose, and lip. Orange spiked hair tops it all off. She blocks my way as I hear her say, "Wow! Cool haircut!" At first, I glance around to see whom she is talking to and then realize I am the only one standing there. Slowly, her hand reaches out to rub my head, and I hear her say, "Isn't bald fun?"

Every person in the store turns to look at me. So much for darting down an aisle to avoid being seen. I see my favorite checkout person out of the corner of my eye. She doubles over in laughter, and I begin to chuckle. I get my soda and head back home.

Suddenly, a sadness comes over me, and my hands begin to tremble on the steering wheel. I go straight from the car to my bathroom mirror and stare myself down. I want to see what it is that girl saw. Only I don't see cool, and I don't see fun. I see pain. Sorrow. And for the first time since my diagnosis, I see my own death.

For three days, I cry and feel sorry for myself. On this fourth day, the mirror reveals the smiling face of a seventeen-year-old with orange spiked hair. I rub my hand across my bald head. This is real. The wig is a facade. The wig allows everyone to pretend that I am well. But I am not well. I am fighting a fight that most people will never have to fight. My life belongs to the hospital, the doctors, the drugs. Unlike this disease, wearing the wig is something I have control over. I want my bald head on display for the world to see-a symbol of my independence and strength.

When my kids arrive home from school, I run to the top of the stairs and stand tall with my hands on my hips. Keaton and Dana stand side by side at the bottom of the stairs, and they both stare up wide-eyed, jaws slack at the sight of me. "What's with the attitude, Mom?"

"You see this?" as I point to my head. "This is my badge of courage, my bald badge of courage. Today, I became cool."

With the infinite wisdom and sensitivity of an eleven-year-old, Keaton shrugs off his backpack and lets it hit the floor with a thud, and says "Weird, Mom."

A couple of weeks after I've lost my hair, I really like my new image. Not just the image but the new me. For the first few days, Hal didn't like me going without my wig. I think my bald head reminds him that I am sick, that I have something more than the flu. It is much easier for him to pretend I am well if I am wearing my wig.

Other people don't say much. They generally steal glances when they think I'm not looking and wonder among themselves why I don't wear a wig. In public, small children stare with their mouths wide open and adults act as if I have become invisible. If adults look directly at me at all, they tend to focus on my ears. Teenagers almost always make direct eye contact or ask questions.

On a shopping trip with Dana one afternoon, our checkout clerk is about sixteen with cropped hair, and, like the teenager in the grocery store, she has piercings everywhere. Without warning, she reaches across the counter, rubs my head, and says, "Isn't it great not to have hair?" My eyes open wide with surprise. After a short laugh, I realize this is the second time a teenage angel has rubbed my head. Must be a sign of luck.

The three-hundred-dollar wig seldom touches my head. Occasionally, family pressure pushes me to appear "normal," and the wig goes on. We are putting an addition on our house, and when applying for the construction loan, Hal was afraid the bank would turn us down if they thought I might not live long enough to pay it off! So the wig went on to impress the bankers.

My bald badge of courage allows people to see who I really am. No more facades. No more pretending to be the super mom and super executive with no fears. If I die in six months, those people in the store are not going to reject my children or my husband because I didn't wear a wig. Those people aren't going to come to my funeral anyway. Dana says, "Go for it, Mom." Keaton pretends not to care one way or the other, but I overheard him saying to one of his curious friends that his Mom's bald head is a little weird.

Most important of all, I have given myself a good laugh. I have taken charge of my life and my identity. I am starting to be a person who is more worried about a happy life for me and my family than the opinions of complete strangers.

The amazing thing to me about my hair loss is that I have lost every hair on my body. For some naive reason, I thought I would lose only the hair on my head. But when I look down and see that my arms and legs are bare and my eyebrows are gone, I am reminded that my entire body is being affected by this process. Some people tell me bald is now chic. Chic or not, my baldness is a symbol of truth. While my life now belongs to others–the hospital, the drugs, and the doctors–the decision to wear or not wear the wig is mine and mine alone. To me, it represents strength and determination. My strength comes from within, and I live with a newfound peace of mind that no matter what happens, I am making this journey with integrity, courage, and a renewed desire to connect with others.

Although my hair will grow back, I will never be the same person again. I will always see myself bald. I will always see my symbol of truth and courage. And I will always remember to look at others and see what is the truth for them. No matter how much hair I have, I will see my baldness.

For the first time in recent memory, I begin inviting those around me to participate in my life. Slowly, people begin to step into my world and heart, and unlike the old Lynne, I let them in.

Chapter Twelve

Invisible healers soften my journey
without even knowing they have
entered my life.

The peculiar thing about cancer is you don't really feel it. You feel the treatments, but in the early stages, you do not feel the disease. For two years, cancer inhabited my body, and I did not have an inkling. When I initially told Dr. Holmes the lump was not painful or sore he said, "That's a clue because malignant lumps seldom are."

The treatments are horrible. I am tired and winded most of the time. Climbing a flight of stairs feels like running straight up the side of a mountain. However, I look healthy. The flu or a bad cold makes me look a lot worse than cancer does. Cancer is more insidious. The only allusion to something wrong is my baldness, some bloating, and a slight yellow tinge to my skin brought on by the chemotherapy. It isn't obvious like being in a wheelchair or hacking and sneezing from a cold. For the majority who wear wigs, the clues are subtle and take a trained eye to spot.

Sometimes I find myself wanting people to feel sorry for me or at least know what I am experiencing. I want them to say something–anything–like, "Gee, I hope you'll be okay." When people ask me "How are you?" I feel foolish saying, "Just great." I am not just great. I am sick. I am scared, I am tired. People inquire after my health like their mothers taught them, but they are repelled by an honest answer.

Perhaps the original intent of the question "How are you?" is to judge the state of a person's immediate health and the effect their proximity could have upon you. A response such as, "Lousy, I have the plague" would cause the person inquiring to run as fast as possible in the opposite direction. "Lousy, I have cancer" tends to elicit the same response. Sometimes I want people to look me in the eye and say something. How hard is that? I want to yell at people. "Look inside of me! I'm not what I appear to be!" On the other hand, there are the times I get irritated when people sympathetically acknowledge my plight. I live in this state of duplicity. Half the time, I am ready to give in and put on the wig and the makeup and pretend with the rest of the world, and the other half of the time, I am ready to stand bald and unapologetic.

I am really confused by this disease and this process. Every time I see the oncologist, I ask her whether I still have cancer in my body. She tells me she doesn't know. Does that mean cancer is a part of my past, or are the cancer cells still running through my body?

People say I look healthy and well, yet I feel sick. I'm always tired. I'm always nauseated. Having a person with a bad cold who looks like death warmed over and who may be only weeks away from death looking healthy and appearing to live a normal life is incongruent.

The chemotherapy treatments come every three weeks. They are no longer the exception. They are the routine. Words to describe them simply do not exist. "Horrible," "terrible," and "awful" are the most extreme words I can think of. As far as I am concerned, beets and eggplant are horrible, terrible, and awful. Chemotherapy is a thousand times worse. The treatments themselves require four long hours in that hospital recliner, immediately followed by cotton brain and rubber legs. Thirty hours after each treatment, I return to the hospital for a second dose of anti-nausea drugs. The remainder of that first week is spent horizontal. I live on water and the kindness of family and friends. The second week brings gradual recovery. My brain begins to function again, and I am out of bed for four- and five-hour stretches. The third week, I feel pretty good, and except for getting extremely tired, I can do most everything I did before: work about three to four hours a day, take the kids to their various lessons, and run some errands.

Many people have come to help. Some are complete strangers who have heard I need help and offer their time and care. I am amazed at how many people reach out. Friends drive me to the hospital, a different friend each time. Sometimes they sit with me during the treatment; sometimes they leave. Often someone else drives me home, and when I arrive home, my house is transformed. Someone has changed my sheets and cleaned the bathroom. Someone else has tackled the vacuuming and the kitchen clutter and has left a casserole for my family's dinner.

I used to see illness as something that interfered with my routine. I never imagined it was something that would become my routine. I never thought my life would revolve around illness. I didn't want the treatments to begin, yet with the fourth fast approaching, I'm not sure I want them to end. They feel safe. Something that was so unpleasant is now something I look to as a source of protection, a means to keep the demons away, to stop the cancer spreading. The thought of stopping the aggressive chemotherapy in a few months is almost as scary as starting it.

What was once scary has become the norm. The days and weeks and months have taken on a sameness. I have learned that going through life is not like being on an interstate highway traveling sixty-five miles per hour all the time. I got off the superhighway. This journey has turned into one of those back roads with mud and bumps and ruts and beautiful scenery along the way. It is slower than the fast lane. It feels safe, and the routine of the treatments feels like a protection, a cocoon.

I am a person of action, and as long as I am on the aggressive treatments, I feel I am actively fighting the cancer. I know I will be on a milder program for the next five years, but will it be enough to keep me well? Will it protect me? Will I have to start worrying about what I wear again? Will I have to return to the hectic corporate life of travel and constant meetings and ninety-hour work weeks? Can I stay bald?

In the beginning, I was afraid of who I would become, into who I would evolve. Now I am afraid I will lose this new person I have become.

I am afraid that once the trappings of cancer are removed, I will go back to where I started.

I'll miss the wonderful people–friends, doctors, nurses–who have become so much a part of this journey. They care about me and for me. These relationships are helping me to heal as much as the treatments. And when the treatments end, the relationships end. The relationships that have helped keep me whole. More change. Then there is the whole question of whether I will even be cancer free when this is over, and if so, will I remain safe from this disease?

During an exam before my fourth treatment, my oncologist checks the mottled flesh of my wrists and says the nurses are frustrated and complaining. "They can't find a vein," she says. "The drugs have collapsed them." My last treatment was extremely painful. Two nurses spent ten or fifteen minutes poking my wrists and trying to find a decent vein. Once they found one, it took an eternity to get the medicines in.

"We'll need to install a catheter in your chest," my oncologist says. "That way, the drugs flow directly into the large blood vessels near the heart."

My feet and hands turn icy. "Won't that damage my heart?" She assures me it won't, but she says that the installation of the catheter does have to be done under general anesthesia.

That evening, I give Hal the news about my upcoming surgery and ask him to please make sure he can take me to the hospital. "Not a problem," he mumbles from behind the newspaper. "Hal, it's this Thursday. The day after tomorrow." He crosses an ankle over his knee and rattles the paper to smooth out the pages.

Sitting in the family room Wednesday night, he lowers the paper and says, "By the way, I have some bad news. My boss expects me to go to California tomorrow. They had a meeting already scheduled before I knew about your surgery."

"What? You can't go to California!" There is not an ounce of moderation in my voice. "You promised you'd take me to the hospital tomorrow to have the catheter put in. How am I supposed to get there? It's 9:00 at night, and I'm supposed to be at the hospital at 6:00 a.m.!"

Looking at me from behind his newspaper, Hal says, "Take a taxi."

Believing he is serious, I shout, "What? Take a taxi? Are you serious? I'm going to have surgery, and you want me to take a taxi to the hospital? Well, guess what? I'm not taking a taxi to the hospital. You can cancel your trip."

He chuckles and says, "Calm down, dear. You said this was a minor procedure, so I have made arrangements for Larry to take you. He'll pick you up at 5:30."

"Ha, ha," I say rather sarcastically. "What kind of warped sense of humor have you developed during this process?"

Intellectually, I understand his life at work cannot stop because of me. I also know that he is operating from a place of fear and is just as happy to have a reason to disappear. Aren't we all coming from a place of fear? He is not even aware he is doing this. He really believes his meetings take precedence over driving me to my appointments, his logic being anyone can drive, but no one else can explain his product design, which is true—but still. Sometimes I wish he would just drop everything, but then the bills arrive, and I am grateful he has such a good job.

My friends and my family get angry with him, but I understand how much he cares and how afraid he is of losing me. Like father, like son. Given Hal as a role model, it is no wonder Keaton did not want to visit during my surgery. After being married to him for twenty years, I can predict Hal's fear and his reaction to it. As Nick pointed out, Hal's behavior fits a long-established pattern. I believe that when we are in any type of relationship, we have to reevaluate it every so often to make certain it is still relevant to our life. And I think we have to look carefully to make sure we are looking at the other's intentions. I believe we tend to judge ourselves by our intentions, and yet we judge others by their behavior. I don't think my family understands Hal's intentions, but I do. Besides, maybe it is Hal's detached attitude that helps me keep my own fear in check and brings a sense of normalcy to my life.

Thursday dawns, and my neighbor picks me up early so I can arrive at the hospital by six. After waiting around for an hour or so, they finally take me to the operating room. I ask the doctor why they have to give me a general anesthetic and put me to sleep. "Can't you do this under a local anesthetic instead? It doesn't seem like much of an operation to me." My surgeon chuckles his usual chuckle and says, "Normally, people are nervous and prefer being knocked out. If you'd rather have a local, we can do it that way. I'd also like you to take a tranquilizer because it will help you hold still. We don't want you moving around once we start."

"Sounds good to me."

The operation is fascinating. A live x-ray is projected on a big screen and shows the progress of the catheter. Snaking its way from the lower left side of my right breast to my shoulder, it takes a left turn under the skin to the sternum and then trails down into the vena cava and makes the shape of a giant backward question mark. All the while, the surgeon describes the process, and it's as if I'm watching a documentary on television.

Because I haven't had general anesthesia, I am back in recovery for an hour and then home by noon. In front of the bathroom mirror, I stare at the end of the catheter. Sticking out of the lower corner of my right breast is a coil of rubber tubing about one-eighth of an inch in diameter and eight inches long. On the end of it is a blue plastic valve about an inch long with a screw cap. When this cap is removed, the catheter serves as a direct pipeline into my blood stream. When not in use, the tubing is coiled up and taped to my chest.

I have to clean and flush the catheter with saline once a week. My hands shake the first time I lay out the swabs, alcohol, and saline. I carefully swab the area where the tube enters the skin with alcohol and then swab iodine in a circle about two inches in diameter around the same opening. Next, I slowly unscrew the cap and pick up a syringe. The end of the syringe fits into the end of the catheter, and I gently squirt the saline into the tube. I can feel the cold seep through the tubing. Screwing the cap back on the tube, I let out my breath and realize another new skill has been added to my repertoire. I soon perform this ritual as casually as I brush my teeth.

Are the treatments worth it? Many times I ask myself whether I'd do this again. Am I going to survive because of my decision to go ahead with these treatments, this hell on earth? Nausea now starts two days before each treatment. Just thinking about it makes me gag. Passing the liquid food supplements in the grocery store makes me gag. Yet, I will crawl through hell to live. Only six months of this aggressive treatment, and then one way or another, it will end. I've lived fifty years. I want another fifty. Six months is a blink of an eye, a second in eternity. I can do anything for six months.

This disease won't win. It can't win. Only I can win. And then I wonder, am I winning? What's the score? Lynne: 1, cancer: 0? The son of my friend Lee died of AIDS. He was sixteen, and I am fifty. If I die today, I have experienced three times more life than he did. When I begin to think that hell is mine alone, I realize that I have a chance. I can fight. I can win. Ben could not. I have been given the gift of taking a unique journey—a wake-up call to truly experience life, whether it be for another fifty years or only one year. Yes, I can crawl through hell. Life is worth it.

Because my treatments are so awful, I always make certain I schedule something I enjoy five days afterward. The day usually starts with a malted milk shake. I've gained thirty-five pounds, but at this point, I don't care. The day also may include anything from a reading at the local bookstore to a trip to the park with Sheba and Snookers. Throughout this illness, these dogs have been a constant, steadfast at my side regardless of how the peopled landscape changes, especially Sheba. Sometimes I worry she is spending too much time with me. She seems to want nothing more than to lie by me and rest her head in my lap for the occasional ear rub.

Today is a warm October day full of blue sky and rolling green grass, a day perfect for the park, but the park is not going to do it. I am itching to get away. I need time alone, time to reflect and mentally heal. Cancer has sent tentacles throughout my soul, and while my body may be recovering, my spirit is dying. Because I'm between treatments, I decide, on the spur of the moment, to go to the mountains, to Holden Village. This Lutheran retreat center in the Northern Cascade wilderness is my safe haven, the place I go to refresh and heal my spirit. Hal has rearranged his schedule so he can take care of the kids, and off I go.

Getting to Holden is an adventure under normal circumstances. First a seven-hour drive to the small town of Chelan, Washington, and then a two-hour boat trip up a forty-mile lake, followed by a twelve-mile trek on a dirt road back into the wilderness in a rickety old bus. Because I can't make the long drive, this trip is much more complicated.

First I fly to a Seattle. Just maneuvering through the SeaTac airport is a chore. Long, long corridors that I have literally run through in the past now seem miles and miles long. Breathless, I arrive at the gate to catch the small commuter plane to Wenatchee, Washington, a town about fifty miles from Chelan. No sooner do I sit down than the gate agent announces the plane is ready for boarding. "Please go down the steps and across the tarmac," he says. The two hundred yards of tarmac between terminal and plane shimmer slick from a mid-morning shower. The plane seems just beyond reach like an oasis in the desert. Crowding down the terminal stairs with the rest of the passengers, I am determined to keep up, but bit by bit, I lose ground. Breathless, I stop every five or six feet to regroup. The gap between me and my fellow passengers widens by the moment. By the time everyone else is ascending the aircraft stairs, I am only halfway across the tarmac. A sympathetic airline employee zooms up in a cart and offers me a ride. Grateful, I hop in.

Once in Wenatchee, I endure a two-hour bus ride to the town of Chelan. The bus drops me off in the center of town, five blocks from the motel. Because the boat leaves only once a day, in the early morning, I have to spend the night. Chelan has no taxis, so I drag my suitcase behind me as I feel the ache of my skin pulling from around the catheter no matter how careful I try to be. Deflated, I begin to wonder at the sanity of making this trip alone. If I couldn't make it across the tarmac to the plane, how am I going to walk five blocks, with suitcase in hand? Lynne, you idiot. When are you going to admit that you simply can't do all the things you used to do?

After half a block, I am breathless and set down my suitcase. The streets are quiet and as slow moving as I feel. The curve of the lake just off between the buildings gives me a moment of peace, a reminder of why I'm putting myself through this journey. Just as I am about to resume my trek, an old man, a local farmer, with hands the size of small skillets wrapped around his old truck's steering wheel, sees my dilemma and offers me a ride. Feeling very safe in this small town, I gratefully accept his offer. Thank you, God, and thank you whoever you are for taking the time to stop and help a stranger. This man and others like him have become what I call my invisible healers.

Invisible healers soften my journey in ways they cannot imagine. A touch, a smile, a nod, a song–some small act that fortifies me. Within the context of going about their own lives, invisible healers leave little bread crumbs behind, not realizing they are lifelines, not realizing a small starving bird is trailing behind, picking up the crumbs and using them to stay alive. These healers have no idea of their contribution to my healing process. They pass through my life, often not even knowing they have entered it. They come and go without a blink, like angels sent from God.

After a night of rest, I rise early, have breakfast, and start my two-block pilgrimage to the boat. The manager of the motel sees me trudging through the parking lot and offers me a ride. Another invisible healer has just passed through my life.

From this point, the trip to Holden Village involves a two-hour boat ride up the length of Lake Chelan. About half an hour into the trip, all roads lining the lake stop and turn into mountain hiking trails. This is literally the end of the road.

An hour and a half later, the boat comes to a small landing with a forest service road that winds up into the hills. Once a day, the Village greets those disembarking and ushers them into an ancient school bus. Then begins a one-hour bumpy and dusty drive up winding switchback roads. As the creaky bus winds further and further from civilization, the voice of my oncologist summons up a small twinge of guilt. "We don't want you more than an hour and a half from a hospital," she said.

"Oh, I'll be just fine," I told her. "They can bring in a helicopter and get me to a hospital easily in that amount of time. Besides, Holden has an RN on staff who has been an oncology nurse." The part about the nurse is true. The part about the helicopter is sketchy. In reality, the forest service has to be contacted, and, if the weather conditions are right and the helicopter is ready to go from a nearby location, then, and only then, they can fly in and airlift someone out. It is not easy, but I saw it done once when someone fell high up on the mountain.

In my heart, I know that nothing bad will happen to me at Holden. My family and I have been coming here for almost twenty years. There is an intimacy in coming to here, a safety I find in few other places.

After twelve miles of being jostled in the rattling bus, we arrive at this remote spiritual retreat center deep in the forest. In the summer, Holden Village accommodates several hundred guests, but this week in early October, the village consists of only the seventy staff members and one other person, who like me, is on a personal retreat. The Village has no telephones, no radios, no television, and only an occasional three-day-old newspaper. It is remote in the truest sense of the word. If you cannot look into your soul here, you cannot do it anywhere on this planet.

The other guest happens to be a grief counselor and Lutheran minister whose wife has just died. He, too, is using this time to reflect and recover. We soon become friends and start having long fireside chats. I begin talking about my death. He understands and doesn't try to stop me with platitudes or false statements such as, "Oh, you're going to be just fine." This afternoon, we talk about my funeral. "I have it all planned and have pictured the entire event. As a matter of fact, it is going to be so fabulous that I don't want to miss it. Maybe I should have it while I'm still alive. Has anyone ever done this before? I think it's a shame that we don't get to hear all the wonderful things people say about us when we die. We should change the tradition and celebrate people's lives before they die, not after."

I go on to tell him my innermost deepest secret, my fantasy of throwing in the towel. "What would happen if I just stopped all this fighting? Sometimes I feel I can't let up for one second. Thoughts of my kids and family push me on. But other times–" I lean back into the overstuffed lodge chair and spread my hands palms up. My gaze shifts away from the minister to the stone hearth. "Other times I'm just so tired. It would be a relief to just end it now and stop all this hassle. I get really confused about this. How can I fight for my life one minute, swearing that I'll crawl through hell to live, and then want to give up the next minute?"

"Why won't people let me talk about the possibility of death?" I ask. "I know they mean well, but all I get is denial and feeble reassurance that I'll be okay. I have a fatal disease. I may not live. Do people think if I don't talk about it, it won't happen?"

This man of God listens patiently, understanding everything I am saying. Although my counselor, Nick, has been outstanding in letting me talk about the dying process, this is the first time I've actually spoken about my thoughts of giving up the struggle out loud. I wonder whether this minister has any idea what a healer he is to me right now. He's visible in that he is present in the here and now, but he is also invisible in that once we leave Holden, it is unlikely our paths will cross again.

My week at Holden goes by rapidly. I spend hours and hours reflecting on my entire life as I write continuously in my journal and read book after book about the dying process and survival stories. I pray in evening vespers every night. "Please, God, help me cope with this disease. Help my family." And then, picturing the kids and Hal without me, I can't help but sneak in "Please make me well."

Leaving Holden to return home, I realize how many healers enter my life almost daily from many different directions. They write songs and books telling their stories. They give quick hellos in parking lots. The other day, a woman I had never seen before came up to me and asked whether I'd been sick. She saw my bald head and wanted to wish me well. These invisible healers are children, neighbors, business executives, and street people. They come in all colors and shapes and from all walks of life. They are you and me, and their impact lasts forever. One day, someone told me that I had been an inspiration with my story. I was? When? How? I thought I was only telling my story. Is is possible that I, too, am an invisible healer?

Chapter Thirteen

I know that I'll be here tomorrow.

As the chemotherapy treatments progress, my energy level decreases almost daily. My white blood counts are also dropping quite dramatically, and I am very disappointed this week when my treatment had to be postponed because my cell counts are at a critical level. My immune system is extremely weak, and exposure to normal germs becomes dangerous. I have always been able to fight off colds and flu, yet with little warning, a cold turns into pneumonia and leaves me flat on my back in hopes I don't have to be hospitalized.

Days in bed pass slowly, giving me lots of time to drift in and out of thought. One thing my mind stumbles upon is the fact that I used to smile a lot—even when I didn't really want to smile. Many times I was smiling on the inside, and it didn't show on the outside. "Smile," people would tell me. "You look like you're frowning." But from the day I was told I had cancer, I stopped smiling. I simply have not been able to smile. I cannot laugh. I'm not sad all the time. It's just that the joy has been squeezed out of me. I've had no desire to smile since my life has become a day-to-day struggle for survival, an endurance test.

I am tired. I am scared. I do not enjoy this journey I am on. I don't want to be on it. My family doesn't want to be on it, but we have no choice. It is not just my journey, but it is also a family journey. Cancer is our disease, not just my disease.

Family counseling with Nick helps all of us realize that we each have our own way of handling the scare and the process of this disease.

Each family member's anger, fear, and denial make much more sense—everything from Hal's being too busy to take me to my treatments to Keaton's refusal to visit me in the hospital. Cancer affects each person differently, and losing my ability to smile is one of the many fallouts.

My profession, sales and marketing, encourages false smiles. Always on stage and smiling on command regardless of how I feel. Too much time putting on an image. Smiling when I am supposed to smile. Always trying to please others. Always trying to do the appropriate, polite thing. Once cancer struck—poof—my smile flew out the window. Now I no longer have the energy or desire to pretend. I am too tired to waste any energy on pleasing others just for the sake of politeness. Besides, I might die soon, and why should I bother? They aren't going to come to my funeral anyway.

Sometimes I wonder whether I will ever smile again. Will this disease kill me before I remember how to smile? A month went by and then two—no smile. These are sad times, dreary times, crying and hurtful times. Smiles don't belong. Is my smile gone forever or just misplaced? Knowing that my smile is not lost has become important to me.

A scheduled check-up lands me in Dr. Holmes's office on a dim and stormy December day when finding a reason to smile is hard enough even without cancer. I sit on the edge of the exam table as I swing my pale feet and wait for Dr. Holmes. I hope the pneumonia will not give him cause to demand I be hospitalized.

Today the view across the Willamette River to the wooded ridge beyond is obscured by low clouds and driving rain. The river, muddied by days of runoff, is a gray-brown matte. It's amazing to think that underneath all this weather the view remains the same pristine view I first saw. Circumstances have only temporarily altered it. Maybe it's the same with me and cancer.

The room's interior, though generic, is positively cheerful by comparison with the storm outside. The obligatory crinkle paper, clean and white, stretches over the exam table. The same little stool on wheels shows some wear along the edge of the aqua vinyl seat. The stainless-steel sink is scrubbed clean as is the counter, but hung on the wall next to a chart of the musculoskeletal system is something I don't remember seeing—a calendar with a picture of one bright shining buttercup nestled in a field of purple flowers. Suddenly and completely unexpectedly, I know where my smile is. It is in the buttercup.

Dr. Holmes enters the exam room, his head bent to my chart, and before he can even look up, I say, "I want that picture. That one of the purple flowers with the one shining buttercup." He looks up from my chart over the top of his glasses. He glances over his shoulder and motions to a photograph of a field of flowers. "This picture?" he asks.

"Yes," I say, my voice emphatic. "That buttercup has my smile. I thought it was gone forever, but here I've found it again."

He sets my chart on the counter; the corner of his mouth lifts in a wry grin, and then he takes the calendar from the wall and carefully tears off the picture. He hands it to me. "Here," he says. "It's yours. Don't ever let it be said that I stole someone's smile."

As soon as I get home, I go straight to the bedroom and hang the picture of the buttercup right across from our bed. Everyday, it sees the tears in my eyes and says, "It's okay, Lynne. I understand. I have your smile. Someday you'll need it again. In the meantime, know that it is safe with me. It will stay pretty and cheerful and happy. I'll keep it shiny, safe, polished, and healthy. When you're ready, I'll let it go."

I've come close a couple of times, but the time was not right. The tears are still there. When I am ready to take care of it with the same gentleness and understanding of the buttercup, then, and only then, I will take it back again.

What a relief to know my smile is safe. Now I tell my friends that if they see a buttercup, it is me smiling at them.

I know my smile will return just as the buttercup promises. It is safe for now, and when I take it back, it will be cozy and familiar like slipping on an old pair of house slippers. Every buttercup holds not just my smile but the smile of every man, woman, and child who has ever had to endure the pain and sorrow of cancer. They, like me, are patiently waiting for the day when their smiles will return.

Almost daily, I meet people with cancer who look the picture of health even a short time before death. Often, these people are active and full of life; they wring the most out of every moment. These are my teachers, my mentors. At one of my treatments, I meet a man with liver cancer who is having such a good time living that the three months his doctors gave him have stretched into two years. Then there is my church friend Allen, a pediatrician riding a five-year remission from leukemia–a long enough remission to develop a false sense of security. Allen always asks about me but quickly brushes aside any concern about himself.

Recently, Allen's cancer returned. A suitable match for a bone marrow transplant cannot be found. I am devastated. He, however, goes on hikes. What kind of fatal disease is this anyway? Dying people going on hikes? Have some of the hikers I've passed on the trail actually been dying of a fatal disease? Do average people have any idea how many people they encounter who are terminally ill but look "fine" to the casual eye? There is no logic in how this disease functions. No logic to the fact that Allen managed a five-mile trek a few days before he died.

I once read a story describing a shipwreck with a lone thirteen-year-old survivor. When asked how she made it to shore, she said, "I kept telling myself, just swim one more stroke. I knew I could take just one more stroke." Each chemotherapy treatment, each day, is like one more stroke. I have a mental scorecard, and I mark slash marks in the "win" column.

I am obsessed with knowing whether the treatments are working. After six months and eight treatments, will I still have cancer cells running around my body? Has the chemotherapy already killed them off, or are they lurking somewhere waiting to spring into action? My doctors say they can only play the odds, and statistically, after all of the treatments, they assume the cancer cells are dead. Doesn't sound very scientific to me. I want to know whether I am winning or losing the game, yet no one can tell me. Each day has become an exercise in faith, and I must trust that I am being guided every step of the way.

Eighteen weeks into this process, I have six of these nasty treatments behind me and two ahead. I've been to the hospital so many times that the last time I asked the admitting clerk whether they give frequent-stay points!

The physical effects of the chemotherapy have taken a toll on my body and psyche. I am at my very worst. As treatment number seven nears, resentment builds to the point where my defiant three-year-old digs in her heels and shouts, "No. I don't want to go. Don't make me do this again." I am sick and tired of being so sick and tired following each treatment. So sick and tired that I decide that not only I, but also all of us, need to get away.

That night after Dana and Keaton are in bed, Hal and I are snuggled down in our usual spots in the family room, each in our own chair, the table lamp between us, with Snookers and Sheba softly snoring between the two foot stools. Hal is buried behind the business section as usual. "Hal," I say, "it's February, it's cold, and I'm ready to get out of here. I have a great idea. Let's go to Disneyland this weekend. This is Thursday. I can call the airlines and see whether we can get free flights using my frequent-flier points. We could leave tomorrow afternoon."

Hal lowers his hands, which causes the paper to slowly crumple in his lap, and he looks at me as if I have lost my mind. "Tomorrow? People don't just go to Disneyland tomorrow. Disneyland is fifteen hundred miles away. It's something you plan for. It's something we can do this summer."

"Hal, do I need to remind you that I may not be here this summer? But I know that I'll be here tomorrow. Think of it this way. This trip is courtesy of cancer and United Airlines. No point letting those miles go to waste. United Airlines is not going to immortalize me because I died with two hundred thousand miles in my account, and they certainly aren't going to mourn my death. Actually, they might, considering all the business they will lose. If we can get the free seats, I say we go." One call to the airline, and we got the tickets!

The next day, while talking with a friend, I hear her say, "You can't be so active. You should rest. Disneyland and wild rides may not be a very good idea. You have to take care of your health." I hear this all the time: "You can't do this. You can't do that. You have cancer."

"Huh?" This makes no sense to me. "What could be worse than dying from cancer? What could possibly happen to me that is worse than what is already happening? How am I going to harm my health?

What health?" I wave away her concerns and return to my excitement about surprising the kids with the upcoming trip.

Saturday morning arrives, and we wake Dana and Keaton. We say, "Get dressed. We have a plane to catch. We're going to Disneyland today."

Keaton says, "Sure, Mom. What happened to you? Did your cancer go to your brain? Dad, I think Mom's gone crazy."

At Disneyland, I stand in the same line at Space Mountain I stood in five years ago. Then, I was all shaky knees and sweaty palms. The closer I inched to the front of the line, the shakier and sweatier I became until two places from the front I backed out. Now I'm thinking, how in the world could this hurt me? I'm beating cancer. I've already been on the most fantastic roller coaster ride of my life. This Disneyland ride is nothing to fear—nothing at all.

Hal and I fold into the roller coaster car. Each of us is buckled into a harness similar to something jet fighters and astronauts wear. A metal bar lowers from overhead and locks snug across our laps and forces our feet flat to the floor. Our car kicks into gear with a click and lurches into the darkness. My hands are wrapped tightly around that metal bar. Even if I wanted to, which I don't, there is no turning back now.

For the first few seconds, I can't see a thing. Speed builds on a straightaway to the point where holding my head up is a struggle, so I give in and let it fall back against the car's wall. We hit the first turn, and a night sky opens, a whole solar system of stars, as our car falls away. Its downward plunge uncoils a giddy scream from somewhere down deep, a laughing, crazy scream that has been a long time coming. Whole galaxies zoom into focus and spin off again as we dip and corkscrew through space. I have not felt this alive, this exhilarated, in months. Every cell buzzes. Something bright and shinning pushes into the thick ache at my center. A sliver of yellow pokes through and then floods past the tears and fear and pain until I feel I must be shining as bright as the stars all around, as bright as my buttercup.

For the rest of the ride, I laugh and scream, and when it's over, I insist we all do it again. I haven't felt this alive in months. I may be moving slowly, but I'm just getting warmed up.

The kids look from Hal to me, and Keaton says, "Boy, this is great. Mom's not as grouchy here." "Yeah," Dana says. "It feels like we've been in this sickness bubble forever. This feels like Mom isn't sick at all."

Hal agrees, and we all head back to the Space Mountain line. While we're waiting, Keaton says, "Gee, Mom, maybe cancer isn't so bad after all."

We fly into Portland two days and many roller coaster rides later. We are very tired, but for the first time since cancer, we feel like a relatively normal family. A family that laughs and plays together. A family not being run by the demands of an unpredictable and unreasonable illness.

This trip was the most freeing thing that has happened in a long, long time. I know people have my best interest at heart, yet in trying to protect me, they almost want to stifle my activities. When I hear them say I shouldn't do this or I shouldn't do that, I respond by saying, "This is my process, and I can choose to die anyway I want. When it is your turn, you get to do it your way. My way is to go to Disneyland on the spur of the moment and ride roller coasters."

On the drive home from the airport, we swing by the kennel for Sheba and Snookers. The small office room at the kennel smells of wet dog and medicated shampoo. We all squeeze in, give our name, and wait. The howl and bark of all those dogs pining for their families is unnerving and stirs up a certain amount of guilt about leaving them in a place so similar to the one from which we rescued Sheba. For a dog, there is probably no distinguishing between being dropped at the kennel for a long weekend and being abandoned at the Humane Society for good. I still marvel that Sheba is such a loyal and trusting soul after the family she spent her early years with first abused her and then left her tied to a tree when they skipped town in the middle of a hot July night.

Picking up the dogs from the kennel is something our whole family looks forward to. The rare times we have boarded them, they have burst through the door. Sheba with her whole hind end wagging, so excited to see us that she left unlady-like piddles on the scuffed linoleum. We are all braced for this reaction and anticipate her excitement, but when Sheba comes through the door, she enters at a walk, fully composed, almost stately. The wag in her tail is definite yet subdued. Hal pays the bill while Dana and Keaton help themselves to dog biscuits from the woven basket on the counter. Sheba usually goes nuts for these treats; it's the only time she gets them. But even the dog biscuits do little to spark her interest. She takes the one Dana offers and then drops it on the floor and nudges it around a bit with her nose before she lies down panting. "Maybe she's just sad," says Dana, running her hands over Sheba's cheeks and along her ears. "Yeah," Keaton says. "If I didn't get to go to Disneyland, I'd be sad."

Sheba usually gets herself into the car just fine. Once the tailgate is open, all we have to do is stand back. She leaps in and skids to a stop before she bumps her nose on the back seat. Today, Sheba gets as far as hopping halfway into the back of the van—front feet in, back feet still on the parking pad.

One of Sheba's back legs scrabbles and tries to get purchase on the tailgate to hoist her rear end up, but the tailgate is too high. The only way she'll make it is with a running start or with help. Hal stands behind her and slides his hands under her belly. As tired as we are, there is no denying the sudden surge of adrenaline that shoots through Hal. Near one of Sheba's teats, Hal tells me that close to the groin is a lump the size and hardness of a golf ball. I feel goose bumps go up and down my arms and spine as I reach under Sheba to see what it is he feels.

The moment Hal pulls into the garage, I head straight for the kitchen with Sheba. My fingers gently work around her lump while I describe it to our veterinarian over the phone. Three days, one lumpectomy, and a series of lab tests later, he tells me Sheba has breast cancer. He says he doesn't know how long she has to live, that it could be a long time or a few months. The veterinarian recommends doing nothing and letting the disease run its course.

Immediately, my heart goes out to her, and I know I have to fight for her life. How unfair that this wonderful four-legged gift to the planet should have her life cut short. "We have to help this dog live," I say. "She hasn't had enough love yet to make up for all those years of abuse. She deserves more time. I realize she may not live, but it won't be for lack of trying."

To my amazement, he tells us we have one of the best animal oncologists in the country right in our own backyard.

The veterinary oncologist tells us that breast cancer in dogs is identical to breast cancer in humans and schedules Sheba for a double mastectomy. The affected breast tissue and several lymph nodes are removed and tested. Thank goodness her lymph nodes and the margins are cancer free. She is in stage one.

As a follow-up to surgery, Sheba needs fifteen weeks of chemotherapy. At first I hesitate, knowing Hal will flip at spending an additional $2,500 on the dog. He loves Sheba, but having been raised on a farm, he doesn't view dogs as valuable family members the way I do. So I tell him it will cost half as much as the estimate. He chokes a bit on this, but after much cajoling from me and the kids, he agrees. Then I cheat. Every time I go to the ATM or the grocery store, I skim a bit off the top of the cash withdrawal. The oncologist has agreed to let me make monthly payments with Hal none the wiser. I must admit I have a bit of a guilty conscience, but every time I look at Sheba, I know I have done the right thing.

With Sheba's well-being to focus on and the beginning of her chemo, my final two treatments go by in a blur. Over the course of those fifteen-plus weeks, I nurture her as she develops an aversion to every type of dog food. We both sit on the floor beside her supper dish, she too ill to eat and me coaxing her to nibble. In desperation, I pop a can of liquid food supplement left over from my mother's visit. It's all I can do to hold back from gagging as the thick white liquid covers the bottom of her supper dish. One sniff and those eyes–liquid brown and sad in a way I have not seen since that rainy Saturday at the Humane Society–find mine. Her dish is off the floor and in the sink in a heartbeat. Mother wouldn't approve, but I understand perfectly.

Sheba's chemotherapy treatments use drugs identical to those given to me, and just as I begin regaining my strength, the drugs sap hers. By the halfway mark of her chemotherapy, I have to help her huff and puff up the stairs. I nurture her through a twenty-pound weight loss and through blood counts so low that several treatments are postponed. When she does receive treatments at the oncologist's office, her head rests in my lap. She has no idea what is happening to her, and yet her trust in me is total as I hold her, pet her, and tell her that if love can get me through cancer, love can get her through cancer.

Would another family have treated her? Would another family understand how she feels with each treatment–the unsteady gait and cotton brain that follows? Would they be patient with her wandering away from the yard, at times so disoriented she can't find her way home? Would they put up with her aversion to every brand of food, or would they just give up and put her to sleep?

That rainy Saturday afternoon we visited the Humane Society put Sheba in our path, in my path. Behind the sad eyes, big ears, and brown-black hair stiff with neglect was an extraordinary soul who was treated so badly and had every reason to hate people. Instead, she countered with gentleness and love. Before that day, no one had considered Sheba for adoption. Clearly, our meeting was no coincidence.

Chapter Fourteen

*I'm not brave. I'm scared. I'm doing
what I have to do to survive.*

Eight months later, Sheba and I are both back on our feet and are remaking our lives. She is regaining the weight she lost and scampering with the kids again, while I am losing the weight I gained and am learning to eat better, exercise, and conduct my business life at something less than the speed of sound. My head is covered in a duckling fuzz that seems more odd than being bald ever was. Hal still wishes I would wear my wig but has ceased to comment. With no statistics to support his stand, he is in uncharted territory for a debate. His reaction to my appearance, indeed my entire illness, is emotional, and it bothers him no end to be reminded that this is not a process he can engineer into a tidy solution.

On a follow-up visit, my surgeon brings up having my breast reconstructed. Reconstruction was discussed briefly before my mastectomy. Many women choose to have it done at the same time, but in my case, my oncologist and surgeon advised against it. My cancer was well advanced and, with the tumor found in the chest, they were not at all sure they could tell what was happening in my body behind a reconstructed breast.

To my surprise, breast reconstruction, when done after the surgery has healed, is a lengthy process that takes anywhere from six months to a year. Because the skin has tightened against the chest wall, they must grow additional skin, just as the body grows new skin to accommodate a weight gain. The surgeon inserts an empty pouch into the breast, and then every week for eight to twelve weeks, a small amount of saline is pumped into the pouch and expands the skin on the chest wall. Being a foreign object, the body must accept it, and while rejection is rare, it can happen. At the end of a year, if all goes well, the surgeon constructs a nipple by tying a small piece of breast muscle into a knot and then tattooing a brown aureole.

Being the conformist I am, I think that I am supposed to have this done, just like I was supposed to wear a wig. I let the plastic surgeon talk me into scheduling the surgery. There is no question in Hal's mind that I'll have it. He digs up reams of statistics that support breast reconstruction: the enhanced sense of self-esteem, the diminished sense of loss, the high success rate of the body's acceptance of the artificial breast. I think my breast reconstruction will allow him to pretend that nothing is, or has been, wrong with me.

The information I find is not so optimistic. Rather than coming from doctors and statistical analysis, the information I glean comes from women who have undergone reconstruction. Many women tell me the new breast is very hard and does not at all feel like a real breast. One woman I spoke with actually had her implant burst, not once but twice. The first time, she had surgery to repair it. The second time, she told her doctor just to remove the thing completely.

The biggest issue for me is not my body but a continual feeling of loss, not over the breast but over a lost security and innocence. People don't realize what you lose when you have cancer. Even after you appear to have recovered, they think your only loss has been your health. Everyone tells me this loss is only temporary. "Oh, you'll get over this. I know a lot of people who've survived cancer." But what these well-meaning friends, family, and near strangers don't realize is that in addition to your health, you lose your whole way of life, the whole essence of how you live. Cancer changes you forever. I will never again be the same. I have to exercise more, eat differently, and be ever vigilant for signs of cancer. My body is something I can no longer take for granted. I can never again ignore some little cough or sniffle or overlook a bump on my skin or a cut or a sore. The confidence I used to have in my body is gone, replaced by a low-level, ever-present doubt. Cancer isn't the flu. It isn't something you just get over. No one seems to realize that the tentacles this disease sends out permeate not only my body but also my whole being. It's as if a whole part of my soul is gone–forever.

When do the losses stop? Will they stop with an artificial breast? Does everyone feel this constant loss? Is a deep sense of loss just a part of life that I am only now discovering? Is it like aging? Do old people register a sense of loss over vitality, sight, and hearing–senses that trickle away over time? I'm ready to get old. Those losses occur slowly with time to adjust as you go along. The speed and brutality of cancer intensifies the losses.

I want these losses to stop, to leave me as I am to discover a new sense of peace and wholeness. Will the gain of a new breast bring balance to the losses? Can it possibly replace my old breast and actually make me feel whole? Am I taking a risk having the surgery? I want to know that for every loss there is a benefit. I know now that I am alive. Is that enough?

One morning after Hal and the kids leave, Sheba and I settle into the sunny patch that washes over the kitchen table. Starting this week, the newspaper is running a series about silicone implants, the problems with them bursting, the health risks of leakage, the emotional trauma, physical pain, and expense required to correct procedures gone wrong. I dial my plastic surgeon's number every hour on the hour until he finally returns my call. He assures me that they no longer use silicone and that saline is supposed to be very safe. Running my bare foot over the soft skin of Sheba's belly, my big toe comes to the raised scar of her surgery. She lets out a deep sigh, so content to be just the way she is. She is not the least bit worried about having breasts. She is just content to be alive.

To the surgeon I say, "Sure, that's what they said five years ago about silicone. In five years, maybe they're going to say something's wrong with saline implants."

During these past eight months, I've adjusted to my body. In the mirror, my scars are virtually invisible. It looks as if this is how I was born and this is the way my body is supposed to be. Seeing my chest with no breast is no different than seeing nails on my fingers or two eyes on my face. I simply don't expect to see that breast on my body.

Three days before the reconstructive surgery, I keep turning over the reasons not to have it done. It's painful, and I have had my limit of pain. It isn't going to feel like a real breast. It will take several operations. My oncologist advises against it. I'm sick of the hospital, and most important of all, it sends the wrong message to our children–that a breast is worth discomfort and pain. Enough said–no reconstruction for me. I tell Hal of my decision and am surprised when he supports it fully. "I was trying to give you the positive side only because I thought it was so important to you. If you don't want it, that is okay with me."

Instead, I wear a prosthesis, an artificial breast made of soft rubber designed to feel and look like a real breast. I am amazed at how natural it feels. Because of a phantom itch from time to time, I actually catch myself scratching the rubber nipple. No one can tell my breast is not real. I buy special bras, and the department store sews a pocket in them to hold the breast. When the kids wanted to go to the water park, I was even able to buy a mastectomy bathing suit that accommodates the rubber breast.

Let me differentiate between "accommodate" and "secure." Whoever designed my suit was not thinking about me using water slides, and, of course, the slide the kids hauled me to wasn't just any water slide–it was the highest and steepest in all of Oregon and Washington. With trembling legs, I climbed the scaffolding stairs with Keaton. Dana and Hal opted to watch from the pool deck in front of the slide. Each person ahead of us shot off the end of the slide as if launched from a cannon. First cancer, then Space Mountain, now this.

On my turn, I sat at the top of the slide. I trembled and squeezed my eyes tight before pushing off. The slide was slick, and when I dared to peek, the pool at the bottom approached so fast that all I had time to be aware of was my stomach lodged somewhere around mid-chest. A second later I zoomed off the slide's lip and resurfaced a little disoriented. Eyes round as quarters, the young teenage boy helping people out of the pool said, "What was that?" Slowly, he slipped his hand under this beige thing and pushed it through the water over to me. "Is this yours?" Wide-eyed, I see my rubber breast sitting in the palm of his hand.

Apparently, I hit the water with such force that my rubber breast took on a life of its own, first pulling deep against the elasticity of my suit before launching itself straight up as if being shot from a slingshot. At the edge of the pool, Dana and Hal were doubled over in laughter. When Dana was able to catch a breath, she said, "Don't worry. It was just my mom's rubber breast!"

Will I regret not having reconstructive surgery? I don't think so. Every time I look in the mirror, I admire my body with just one breast. In this body, there is a sense of integrity. Everyday people tell me I'm brave. Brave in the face of chemotherapy, a cure that feels far worse than the disease. Brave to follow my heart to the isolation of Holden Village, a place so far from the medical technology that being there is considered dangerous. Brave to sweep my family off to Disneyland. But I'm not brave. Don't people realize I'm just scared? I'm doing what I have to do to survive. Brave is when you make a decision to do something courageous. I didn't decide to do this. I didn't make a decision to have cancer. I have no choice. What is bravery? Surviving? Is that bravery? I wish I knew.

Listening to story after story of others with cancer makes me realize how little people want to talk about it and how little anyone understands what is happening. If I do nothing else in this lifetime, I hope I can provide answers to some of the haunting questions for others on this journey. I hope that I can listen to their fears about dying, listen to the changes they have had to undergo, and help them hold to their dreams regardless of their outcome.

Since having cancer, I have spent a great deal of time laughing with terminal patients. I have had wonderful conversations about life and the process of death. First with Allen, still hiking a few days before he died, always optimistic. Not in a Pollyanna way but in a way that comes only with deep peace and a knowing of self. Then there was Helen, a dear friend of mine who had non-Hodgkin's lymphoma. She had been in remission for four years when I was initially diagnosed. As I finished my course of chemotherapy, Helen's lymphoma returned, starting with a small lump on her neck and ending with her death six months later. Yet throughout those six months, Helen gave me a gift I will cherish forever. She allowed me to discuss the process of dying. She was open about her pending death and spent many days recounting the memories as she cleaned out her closets in preparation. Two days before her death, we joked and laughed on the phone, and Helen told me she was ready. She had sifted through her life's gifts and said her good-byes. She was at peace.

My life is enriched by people like Helen and Allen, wonderful people who accepted death and were still able to live each of those last days in laughter and a richness of spirit. When Allen and Helen made their transitions, I was able to attend their funerals with a smile. I remembered how much they both enjoyed life right up to the end. To not do so would have been like spoiling the last days of a vacation.

Shortly after Helen's funeral, Dana volunteers me to speak to her high school biology class. I arrive at the school and wonder what I will say and worry about how fast these teenagers will be bored. The first ten minutes are a bit stiff. Following the teacher's introduction, I roll right into the spiel I've prepared about cancer as a disease. I note the stifled yawns, the young woman slouched in the center row whose gum stretches over her tongue repeatedly and whose eyes flit from her many ringed fingers, to ceiling, to floor. The look says, "Interest me–I dare you."

Instead of speaking any further, I open the floor to them. I ask for questions, and, at first, the room is silent. It is going to be a long hour and a half. Dana shifts in her seat and sinks a little. Soon someone blurts out, "Did you lose all the hair on your body or just your head?"

"I lost it all–every hair on my body."

"Does the chemotherapy really make you sick?" a lanky boy asks.

"The cure definitely feels worse than the disease. You can have cancer for a year or more and never know it. When you're on chemotherapy, you know it."

Pretty soon I'm faced with a flood of questions. Yawns have been replaced by eyes sharp, ears intent on my words. "How long does the chemotherapy take?"

"Do they really chop off your whole breast when they do the surgery?"

"Now that you've had the surgery, do you still have cancer?"

"How big is the scar?"

"If they took out the tumors, doesn't that mean you're cancer free? What's the chemotherapy fighting if you're cancer free?"

"Yeah, do you have cancer, or did you have cancer?"

I take each question as it comes and am unable to do justice to some and have to explain to these kids that the doctors do not have the answers, either. They treat cancer patients according to what has worked before and what hasn't, and what works on one patient may fail miserably on another. The girl with the gum has her fingers laced under her chin, with her elbows resting on her desk. Her eyes are glued to me when she asks, "What's it like to know you're going to die?"

What does it feel like to know I'm going to die? The room is final exam quiet. At last I say, "Scary. But not all the time. And, remember, I may not die. Most of the time, I try to focus on the hours and days that I have. And I would like to believe I have many days, months, and years ahead."

They had so many questions the teacher had to cut it off at the end of the hour and a half. It was as if a floodgate had opened for these kids. On my drive home, I reflect on the questions asked by the students—questions adults don't have the nerve to ask.

What made this afternoon so special is that many of these kids have seen grandparents or parents die of cancer, and now they have been unable to get their questions answered. For the first time, someone was taking their fears and curiosity seriously and was talking about the physical process of living with this disease.

When I started this journey, I thought all the change I would undergo would be physical: a different diet, reduced work load, less travel. Change occurring inside my soul never crossed my mind. Change that would transform me into a person who took time to enjoy life and laugh, a person who delights in what God has put me here to enjoy. I am now a spiritual being, and I know that God will provide what I need at the precise time I need it. Sometimes I ask him whether maybe, just once or twice, he could give me what I need in advance rather than at the last minute. Then I remember that God is never late and seldom early.

I do what my heart desires, be it an impromptu trip to Disneyland, milkshakes for breakfast, or learning to ski. Not that learning to ski was on my agenda, but being antsy one Saturday, Dana looked at me and said, "Mom, would you please go skiing with me tomorrow?"

"Dana, I don't know how to ski." We have lived in Oregon for twenty years, and we have never been on the mountain in the winter. I have been too afraid to drive in the snow, and Hal has no desire. Sitting in my warm living room watching television on a snowy weekend is fine with me.

"Mom, I'll teach you." Her eyes, a brown so deep, remind me of trying to resist Sheba's pleading eyes as I eat a sandwich. How can I say no? Even if I break my leg? I can do it. I don't care whether I learn to ski. I only care that I am doing something important for my daughter. I want her to stand at my funeral and say, "Wow, she learned to ski just for me."

The next morning, off we go. She is happy, and I have sweaty palms. The entire trip, I say to myself, "This is for you, Dana. This is a gift from cancer."

Does it matter that it takes me thirty minutes to maneuver my way to the rope tow as I try to walk like a duck? Does it matter that I go only two feet before crashing down in a heap with my daughter folded over in laughter? Does it matter that once we shuffle to the chair lift, they have to stop it because I sit halfway on the arm of the chair and get my ski and pole caught underneath? Nothing matters except I am having fun with my daughter. I am experiencing life at its best. I am fifty-three years old, and I am learning to ski.

I let out a loud whoop and a holler as we glide up the slope in the chair lift. Dana says, "Mom, do you have to tell everyone that you're fifty-three and just learning to ski?"

"Yup! And darn proud of it, too." To complete her embarrassment, a photographer is standing at the top of the lift and is charging twenty-five dollars a pop for pictures—a bargain as far as I am concerned.

So many times people hear their grown children say, "I want to thank my parents for who I am today." I want the reverse. I want to thank my son and daughter, my husband, and my friends for who I am today. I want to say, "Thank you for transforming my life."

Will Dana ever know how much impact that one simple offer of teaching me to ski has had on my life? Will Keaton ever know how his taking my face in his hands when I was down and saying "I love you, Mom" fills my heart with a memory that will stay with me throughout this journey and beyond? Will Hal ever know that, even though I got irritated at his yellow pad and statistics, his confidence in my survival boosted me when I thought I could not go on? Will friends, and even strangers, have any idea how their acts of kindness and invisible healing linger long afterward?

When I was diagnosed, people I least expected stepped forward to be with me on my journey, and people I fully expected to travel along with me disappeared. People I hardly know have stepped forward saying "I can do this for you, or I can do that for you. Please let me."

These healers ask about my health and mean it. They cook, clean, drive me around, do my laundry, sit with me, give me water when I am too weak to get it for myself. They nurture. Then they say "thank you" to me. Why are they thanking me when it is I who should be thanking them? "Thank you" feels ridiculously simple. These people have walked down a path with me that is scary for those who have to go down it, much less those who go down it voluntarily.

"Thank you" is what I say to someone who helps me with my coat or someone who gives me a Christmas gift. But for people who have sacrificed their time and themselves to help me survive and those who have said, "I care," there must be something else I can say or do. Two words, even a hundred words, just aren't enough to convey what is in my heart. Any words, no matter how carefully chosen, seem trite. People gave from their hearts. I could not have made it through without their help. "Thank you" doesn't feel like enough, yet how in the world can I repay them?

I want to buy everyone a present, take them all out for dinner, but there are so many who have stepped forward, sometimes people I hardly know. I wouldn't be able to find them all, let alone afford it.

Maybe all they want is a simple thank you. Maybe by letting go of being so perfectly and completely in charge, so utterly competent, I have made room for others to grow in confidence, to nurture and serve. My heart is truly overflowing, and, usually a person who is never at a loss for words, I can think of nothing to say other than these two simple words: "thank you."

Chapter Fifteen

Regardless of the outcome of this journey,
I have beaten cancer.

The incongruent nature of cancer has taught me about judgment and image: what I see on the outside versus what's going on inside another person. Before cancer, I missed out on enriching my life by eliminating a lot of people on the basis of surface judgment. Now I deal with a disease that is the epitome of conflicts; I appear whole and healthy on the outside while I die on the inside.

Cancer reminds me to look at what really makes a difference in life. This is a long way from worrying about how I am dressed. With the loss of my hair and the decision to forego the wig, I have learned to let go of trying to maintain an image. During my life as an executive and self-appointed "very important person," my clothes came from the finest shops and coordinated perfectly. I wore pearls–real pearls, not anything fake from the local drug store. My shoes, stockings, and purse matched at all times. During the chemotherapy, I was so sick that image made no difference. I got up in the morning and stepped into the first thing I put my hands on, hardly noticing the color or whether it matched anything else I was wearing.

Heading out the door to go shopping one day, Dana looks at me and says, "Mom, you're not going out dressed like that, are you? You're wearing a green and white stripped shirt, purple pants, orange socks, a bright aqua sweater, and a one-dollar plastic watch."

"Am I naked?" I ask.

Dana fills her tiny frame with a deep breath and says, "No, but–"
"But nothing. It works. I am too tired to bother with what looks right. Every store I walk into takes my money; every restaurant I eat in serves me food. The airlines let me fly, and the golf club has not withdrawn our membership."

As I write this, I am wearing a watch of cheap plastic for which inflation now forces me to spend three dollars. It serves as a reminder of a very different person than the one who started this journey. My three-dollar watch reminds me that appearances aren't everything. It reminds me to remember what a snob I was before cancer and that there is no right or wrong side of the tracks, only the tracks, and I am reminded that the gate on the country club not only keeps others out but also keeps me locked in. Putting the brakes on and segregating myself with judgment have opened me to a new world of fascinating people. If I encounter someone I assume I will not like, I look behind the clothes, the hair, skin, eyes, and just plain bad behavior to true intent. Doing that, I often find a person different from the one I first attempted to judge.

Others on similar journeys through the pain and fear and loss of cancer also become lighter emotionally and spiritually. Our bodies may be disintegrating, but our spirits are soaring. Those who have never had cancer or been around chronically ill people have trouble understanding that disease helps us become different people on the inside. I have become a person who looks into her soul and says, "Thank you, cancer, for releasing me."

These days, I follow my heart and live life spontaneously. When I say I live one day at a time, it is a lot different than wearing underwear that has holes and is held together with safety pins because I might end up in the emergency room. It is relishing every moment I have and striking while the iron is hot in every sense of the word.

Afraid there might not be a tomorrow, I do not let any legitimate desire go ignored. Prior to cancer, I held back and deprived myself of what I really wanted, either to please someone else or to avoid criticism. Now, I look at those brownies Dana bakes, and a little voice says, "Go ahead. In six months, you might be dead, and you will be saying to yourself, 'Gee, I wish I had eaten that brownie.'" Is anyone going to come to my funeral and say, "Isn't it nice she was thin and passed up those brownies?" Of course not. How many years have I deprived myself of what I wanted just because someone else might not approve? No longer. Of course, because I don't want to weigh three hundred pounds, I have learned to maintain the philosophy of living for the moment and blending it with common sense.

These days, I step up to the plate if it is in sync with my soul, regardless of what others may think or how well I am apt to perform. I learned that when I'm nervous about my performance, it is because I am worried about other people's opinions. Realizing I may not be around long makes me realize how little their opinions count. I learned how to ski without being perfect on the first try. I did not die of embarrassment but embraced the freedom failure gave me to try again. I'm learning how to hang on tight on the roller coaster and how to let go when the ride is over. I'm learning how to laugh when life makes a fool of me and how to cry when I'm only fooling myself.

I have learned that all the people I encounter are trying to do the best they can, at any given moment, to make it through this journey called "life" in the only way they know how. Status, money, wealth, and outward appearances are meaningless. In each person, I see an ally who wants to lend a helping hand on my journey. Everyone, regardless of material trappings, is equal in the need for acceptance and love. Have you ever noticed that when you look at old people, you only see "old"? You do not see corporate presidents; you do not see ditch diggers. You admire them for their spirit and spunk, not for what they were before growing old.

Once a month, I cook and serve a meal for one hundred and twenty-five homeless men and women who are in the process of trying to get out of their homeless state. People I used to cross the street to avoid, people I used to refer to as "those people," are now people I am honored to have a chance to serve. I now see them as people struggling to live, just as I have struggled. I speak to them. I hear their stories. We laugh together. I enjoy hearing their stories. I enjoy seeing beyond their skin and seeing who they are inside. I enjoy looking behind their eyes.

My reward? They thank me profusely, not in a humbled, subservient way but in the way a peer would say "thank you" at the end of the meal. "Compliments to the chef, madam." They not only help me discover who they are inside, but also they lead me to deeper discovery about who I am.

I knew I had arrived in understanding the equalization process when, one night, I looked up and there standing in the food line, with his plate extended, was my son. "I'm hungry, too, Mom. I haven't had supper." With that, after getting food on his plate, he proceeded to walk over with one of the men, sit down, and eat as if he belonged. My shock gave way to the realization that, as people, he didn't see any difference between us and them. It is the non-equalization that we learn and are taught.

Feeding the homeless isn't an ego trip. I get and want no recognition for this. I just enjoy giving what I can while I walk on this planet. I know it can end tomorrow, that I have only a short time on this earth to help others on their journey as I have been helped on mine. I no longer believe I am better than them. I believe we are all doing the best we can with what we have and what we know.

Five years have passed since my first mastectomy, and the other breast I fought so hard to keep has now been removed. I always knew it was a matter of "when," not "if." During one of my check-ups with the doctor, tests results showed a change in the cells, a change toward new cancer growth. I knew its time had come. Again I chose life. With a sense of sadness and apology, I released my right breast. I thanked it for staying with me as long as possible. As with the left breast, I said I was sorry that I could no longer carry it with me. My breast understood and took its leave gracefully. So I am now the proud owner of two of Nordstrom's finest rubber breasts.

Have I gained from cancer? Has my quality of life improved? Let me tell you one more story, and then I will let you decide for yourself. We joined a very exclusive golf club. Growing up, my family belonged to private clubs, so I have been around this environment all my life, and it fits into my image perfectly. As I have said, before cancer, I lived in horror that I might not use the correct manners, that I might violate their dress codes, both written and unwritten. That, heaven forbid, we would not be accepted by other members. My hands would almost shake if we had to play golf with other members for fear that I might not have the right glove, the right golf sweater or visor, or whatever else the trappings of golf dictated. I can tell you that golf for me was almost a social obligation, not a sport–until now.

Shortly after we joined the club, Hal and I decided that to meet other members, we would participate in what they called "twilight golf," a golfing social event that paired you with several other members in a tournament every other Friday. This was the night of our first social event at the club. Hal had not played golf in more than ten years. As this Friday night got closer, I kept asking him to get out his clubs and at least blow off the dust and see whether he remembered how to hold the club.

I had to go out of town on a business trip and would not see Hal again until Friday night at the country club. While I was gone, instead of practicing, he decided he needed some "new" clubs. Far from the custom-made, graphite shaft, brand name clubs I was using, he went to Goodwill and bought mismatched clubs, some of which had a bit of rust on them. Two of them had wooden shafts, which went out of style at least fifty years ago. All of them had a piece of tape around the top with a five-dollar price tag. Get the picture?

I was not home to supervise and make certain he would present a respectable image, and I can guarantee you I did not see the five-dollar price tags before getting to the country club. Hal was totally oblivious when the bag boy took his golf bag out of the car and put it on a cart. When he was wandering around looking for our cart and his clubs, someone said, "Don't you know what your clubs look like?"

He looked around distractedly saying, "No, I just bought them last night."

On the first hole, he whipped out his rusty two iron with the five-dollar price tag. As soon as the men who were paired up with us saw the club, they shouted, "Where in the world did you get that awful club? It looks like it came from the thirties. And only five dollars?" To add insult to injury, he had on the worst set of clothes that I had ever seen come out of his closet. The one saving grace was he played excellent golf.

The moral to this story is not in his behavior but in mine. Did I withdraw our membership and say "Let's get out of here before they throw us out" on the basis of his image? Even though he played decent golf, did I spend the entire night pretending I didn't know him? While I must admit I thought about both options, I looked at my plastic watch, remembered what was important, and said to myself, "We are who we are. Hal is Hal. This is who he is. He is brilliant. He is very successful. He is a wonderful father and a wonderful husband. He is a caring person. He does not understand or care about image."

While it is important to others, it is not important to him. If the people at the club are going to judge us and reject two people who are kind and sharing, good parents, successful in business, and all-around good, friendly, and honest people, then this is not the place for either of us. If they are not going to take the time to get to know us and what our journey is about, this is not where we want to be.

We were not asked to withdraw our membership. We continue to enjoy playing golf as a family and with other members of the club who have become our friends. We are enjoying life and spending our time in ways that support who we are and the truth we see in life.

Our journey continues, every day in a new way. I wake up and smile, glad to be alive. I look at my children and say, "Thank you, God." I remember that I may not have many tomorrows. I live with no regrets. I follow my soul's desire. I enjoy life regardless of cancer.

You can beat cancer. That's what Bernie Siegel says. His exceptional patients beat cancer—and yet many die. How can this be? How can they beat cancer and die? Doesn't that mean that cancer beat them?

Then it occurred to me. Is beating cancer being told "You're cured"? Or is beating cancer living each day in alignment with your internal truth and living life in a manner congruent inside and out: riding on roller coasters, serving the homeless, laughing at rubber breasts catapulting out of bathing suits, and playing golf with rusty clubs?

Beating cancer is looking it in the eye and still being able to laugh. It is opening my mind to possibilities I usually don't see. Beating cancer is not being afraid of my imperfect body. It is recognizing my mastectomy can't make me ugly. Like the Velveteen Rabbit[3], ugly is possible only to those who do not understand.

Beating cancer is not about statistics on who will live and who will die. Beating cancer is knowing that death is part of life and making choices about how I will live and how I will die. It is being in charge of each day and not being afraid to make my own choices, whether those choices are wearing a three-dollar watch with orange pants or saying no to reconstructive surgery. Beating cancer is thinking as if I will live forever and acting as if I will die tomorrow. Beating cancer is helping Sheba crawl through the same hell I did and now watching her run around the yard with her tail wagging as she chases sticks, rabbits, and deer. To see Sheba's once sad eyes shine and her tail wag when visitors say "What a wonderful dog." I know if I were to ask her whether the treatments were worth it, she would say, "Yes!"

Beating cancer is taking the flying lessons I've always wanted. It is leaving my corporate position and six-figure income because they are out of sync with my soul.

Living each day in alignment with my internal truth, in a manner that is totally congruent inside and out, is beating cancer to the ultimate. Length of life is inconsequential. It is truly the quality of the journey. Beating cancer is standing in a field of purple flowers and seeing the sun shine through one perfect yellow buttercup that is wearing my smile.

When I came to these realizations, cancer became not the enemy but the teacher. Yes, regardless of the outcome of this journey, I have beaten cancer.

About the Author
and Her Family

L ynne Massie resides with her family in Tumwater, Washington, just south of Seattle.

She is an inspirational and motivational speaker who works with people and companies who want to conquer challenges and create more success in their lives. She draws from her years in international business, her encounter with two near fatal illnesses, along with the wonder of making a last minute change in her travel plans to take another flight, after having been booked on Pan Am Flight 103 (which blew up over Lockerbie, Scotland).

Lynne speaks about being a teenager faced with a life-threatening illness and about being a mother who has to tell her young children that she may not survive. When her eleven-year-old son asked her, "Is cancer worse than the flu?" she describes the sense of balance she had to find in order to be truthful with her children and also give them hope.

She and her husband pulled their children into their circle of support and made certain they would always look back on this journey with happy memories, regardless of the outcome.

She goes to the mountains when she wants to rest. She hikes, skis, and takes off on sunny afternoons to play golf. She spends many weekends helping her daughter, Dana, sell her creative, steel, dog silhouettes at AKC dog shows.

Lynne is a career person who has learned that sometimes you just have to go to Disneyland on the spur of the moment and ride the roller coasters.

As a member of the National Speaker's Association, she was winner of both the 2000 and 2002 Oregon Speaker's Association Showcase. If you are interested in having her speak to a group or do a book signing, give her a call at 1-800-755-5399 (or 360-236-7293). If you just want to talk about what you experienced while reading this book or need some support, give her a call.

You may contact Lynne by snail mail, e-mail, telephone, or fax:
Lynne Massie
Turning Point Success
855 Trosper Road #108-310
Tumwater, WA 98512
PH: 1-800-755-5399
FAX: 360-236-7297
e-mail: lynne@turningpointsuccess.com

Dana completed a year of volunteer work at Holden Village, where she endured the rugged North Cascade winter. She has established her own business specializing in steel dog silhouettes and spends time working with rescue dogs. Learning from her mother, she seizes the moment and follows her sense of adventure. She was an exchange student in Japan and traveled with her mother to Korea, China, Taiwan, and Japan and with her father to Greece and Italy. She believes that cancer gave her the gift of a close friendship with her Mom. She says cancer is a journey that never ends and believes it affects many lives for the better.

Keaton is now in college majoring in zoology. He completed a stay in Costa Rica and South Africa as part of the People to People student ambassador program; and, he had the honor of attending a student medical conference at Harvard Medical School. Accompanying his mom and dad, he has visited Australia, New Zealand, Taiwan, Palau, Quam, Hawaii, Greece, and Italy. Originally, at age eleven, when Lynne was diagnosed, he didn't want to visit her in the hospital because he thought the cancer might be his fault. He learned that if he wrote about his fears, he would feel better. To this day, he has continued this practice and expanded it to include painting.

Hal is an electronics engineer currently with a computer and microprocessor company. His hobby is his work, and his work is his hobby. He is entrenched in the Pacific Northwest and definitely prefers the rain to shoveling snow in his hometown of Frankfort, Kansas. He has a brilliant mind and, while currently working in the world of computers, spent many years inventing medical equipment that has had a significant impact on our world: fetal monitors, ultrasonic blood pressure measurement equipment, kidney dialysis equipment, and the world's first self-energizing pacemaker. He was also very instrumental in the development of the Pentium microprocessor systems. He has been awarded more than twenty-five patents throughout his career.

FOOTNOTES

[1] 1993. Paperback. ISBN 0671799312. Mass Market Paperbacks. New York, NY

[2] The Foundation for Inner Peace. Glen Ellen, CA ISBN 0-9606388-8-1

[3] *The Velveteen Rabbit*, Margery Williams, Random House